Nutritious and Delicious

Design and Layout: Anna King
Photography and Food Styling: Estee Gestetner
Book Cover: R. Bakst

Distributed by:
Israel Book Shop
501 Prospect Street
Lakewood, NJ 08701

Tel: (732) 901-3009
Fax: (732) 901-4012

www.israelbookshop.com

Printed in Brooklyn, NY

Nutritious and Delicious

Over 150 whole grain & healthy fat recipes
Sugar-free and No Artificial Sweeteners
More than 115 wheat-free recipes
Kid tested and approved

Naomi Muller

ACKNOWLEDGEMENTS

I WANT TO THANK all my Radiant Recovery friends for their love and support. I want to thank Dr. Kathleen DesMaisons for all her support and knowledge about living a sugar-free life (www.radiantrecovery.com). I want to thank all my friends who graciously tested recipes from this cookbook. You were a huge help to me! And a special thanks to Yehudis for encouraging me to finish this cookbook.

VERY SPECIAL THANKS to my Step Mom, Gail, for a fabulous editing job! And to my brother-in-law, Rabbi Amrom Muller for his brilliant choice of this cookbook's title, it just would not be the same without your valuable input, thank you. Thank you to the Muller boys for tasting all of Mommy's recipes and letting me know which ones were the best. Thank you to Anna King for a really terrific graphic art layout and design. And a huge thanks to Estee Gestetner, who not only took such fabulous photographs, but also dispensed such valuable advice. And without my husband, Rabbi Azriel Muller, and his loving support, encouragement and sage advice, I would not have been able to share this cookbook with anyone, thank you for being my number one supporter and fan. Most of all, I would like to thank Hashem for giving me the gift and ability to cook and to share this gift with others.

DEDICATION

In Memory of
Sara Reva bas Lazer Feivel,
my beloved Mother

and Sara Rivka bas Yitzchak Yosef,
my beloved friend

TABLE OF CONTENTS

FROM THE CHEF'S NOTES...

I HAVE WRITTEN this cookbook to provide great recipes for those who keep kosher and are on a sugar-free (even sugar substitute-free), refined flour-free diet. The recipes are great for children as they have been tested and approved by children. Many of the recipes will be helpful for the kosher diabetic and are ideal for those who suffer from allergies and addictions. All of the recipes are good enough for the whole family to enjoy.

FOR THOSE that are concerned with sugar sensitivity, I just want to make sure that you understand that it comes in "degrees." What might be too sweet for one person will be just fine for another. With that in mind, be advised that not all of the recipes in this cookbook will be suitable for your individual situation. Feel free to alter them so that they suit your needs.

THE DESSERT RECIPES are ones that I have created to appeal to children. My own children were the tasters for the desserts and they enjoyed eating them or they were not included here. Some of them will be a good transition for your children as you wean them off of sugar.

IT IS NOT HARD to cook up some really delicious and nutritious meals. The trick to getting your family used to the new way of cooking is to make gradual substitutions. And sometimes letting them taste the new item, without telling them what is in it, works wonders.

STOCKING YOUR KITCHEN

HERE IS A LIST of some great ingredients you should always have on hand for kosher sugar-free cooking and baking.

Alcohol-free extracts – These wonderfully tasty extracts are sugar and alcohol-free. You can obtain these by checking your local health food store or by ordering them online from www.radiantrecoverystore.com or by phoning 888-579-3970.

Apple Juice Concentrate, Frozen – Keep it in your freezer and scoop out whatever amount you need, covering the container with foil to keep it fresh.

Apple Spread (Butter) – Landau's makes a no sugar added apple spread. It is also great in desserts. There might be some other name brand apple spreads in your local health food store. Be sure to check the label for added sugars.

Bananas – a great sweetener for baked goods and, when frozen, makes a great shake! To freeze bananas, peel them and then put them in freezer bags. Baby food banana, without added sweetener, is the preferred item in many of the baked goods as it gives a very smooth texture. If you prefer to use your own banana, make sure to puree it in a blender or food processor until completely smooth.

Earth Balance Spread – a healthful, non-hydrogenated, no trans fat margarine that you can locate in your local health food store. The tubs are great for spreading and have a fabulous taste. The sticks are super for baking and cooking. The best part is it is pareve (non-dairy).

Light Tasting Olive Oil – This is the preferred oil for all recipes as it has all the health benefits of olive oil with a very light "non-olive" taste.

Sea Salt – Regular iodized salt has dextrose in it. Since we need iodine, I prefer to use sea salt, which naturally has the iodine in it and no added sugars (check the label since not all sea salt has natural iodine).

Vital Wheat Gluten – Is recommended for whole grain bread baking.

Wheat Flour – Many times you can substitute a half cup oat flour and a half cup brown rice flour for one cup of whole wheat flour. On those recipes where we have tested out this alternative for those with allergies to wheat, we have made a notation about substitution.

White Whole Wheat Flour – Is the preferred flour for breads. White whole wheat is a whole grain and is a different type of wheat, called white wheat, than regular whole wheat, called red wheat, and makes really light whole grain bread.

Whole Grain Pastas – These are plentiful and come in all kinds of shapes. The Laundau brand is the best tasting of all the whole wheat pastas. Brauners makes some great tasting whole spelt pasta, including farfel. And for those with allergies, I highly recommend the Tinkyada brand of brown rice pastas. We eat wheat but we really enjoy the Tinkyada pastas and they come out really white looking, too.

Whole Wheat Pastry Flour – Is the preferred flour for baking.

SUBSTITUTIONS

HERE ARE SOME substitutions that might be helpful as you seek to adapt your recipes to a sugar-free, whole grain lifestyle:

❖ 1 envelope onion soup (as a seasoning) = 2 tbsp. dried chopped onion, 2 tsp. salt

❖ Apple juice concentrate = apple juice

❖ Bread crumbs = homemade whole grain bread crumbs or ground nuts

❖ Canned mushroom soup = Imagine Boxed Portobello Mushroom Soup

❖ Canned soup = Imagine Boxed Soup, check label for coverts

❖ Cocoa = carob, I use carob since it has a sweet taste and cocoa is bitter

❖ Graham cracker crumbs = Triscuit crumbs, ground nuts, ground oats

❖ Honey = mashed banana, apple butter, apple juice

❖ Jam = fruit only spread

❖ Matzo meal = whole wheat matzo meal or ground nuts

❖ Raisins/dried fruit (as an addition in baking) = nuts or just omit them

❖ White flour (cakes) = whole wheat pastry flour and in some cases oat flour and brown rice flour

❖ White pasta = whole wheat pasta, brown rice pasta

❖ White rice = brown rice, wild rice

❖ White/brown sugar = mashed banana, apple butter, apple sauce

❖ Wine (savory dishes) = chicken broth, vegetable broth, beef broth

❖ Wine (sweet dishes) = apple juice, orange juice

MOST of the recipes in this book are wheat-free
or offer a substitution for wheat-free.
This symbol

designates recipes that contain wheat
and no substitutions.

BREADS

CHALLAH 🌾

5 lbs white whole wheat or whole spelt flour
3 oz. fresh yeast
1-3/4 cups vital wheat gluten
5-6 cups lukewarm water
2 eggs
1/2 cup light tasting olive oil
2 Tbsp. sea salt
1 egg to brush challah with
sesame seeds, optional

Mix flour and vital wheat gluten in a bowl. In a separate
bowl dissolve yeast in 12 oz. lukewarm water. Let yeast stand
until activated; yeast will start to bubble and foam. Mix eggs,
oil and salt. Add half of flour, half of remaining water and
activated yeast. Mix on low speed and add remaining
ingredients. Knead for 15 minutes until a soft dough is
formed. Take 'challah' according to Jewish law.

Set dough to rise for 1-1/2 hours or until doubled in size.
Cover dough well so it doesn't dry out. I prefer using a
kitchen size garbage bag. Put the dough into the garbage
bag and then close the end. Divide dough into 5 balls. Form
dough into desired shape (braided or unbraided, for
example). Place into greased one pound loaf pans and set
loaves to rise for 45 minutes. Brush loaves with beaten egg.
Sprinkle with sesame seeds.

Preheat oven to 375 degrees. Bake for 45 minutes or until
golden brown and hollow sounding when gently knocked
on bottom. If you make smaller loaves, they require less
baking time.

If you want to freeze, bake challah about 10 minutes less and
put them in a tightly sealed bag (the special challah bags are
the best). Take them out Erev Shabbos and bake them for
10 minutes until the crust is brown.

*White whole
wheat is a whole
grain. It is a
different type of
wheat from
regular whole
wheat and makes
really light whole
grain bread.
The amount of
water used
depends upon the
moisture content
of the flour that
you use. Start
with 5 cups and
add more until
the dough is
moist and elastic.*

ROLLS 🌾

Use the challah recipe, but shape into little round balls. Bake
for about 1/2 hour either on a cookie sheet or in muffin
pans. The number of rolls depends on the size you want.
You can make about 25 medium sized rolls.

BAGELS

1 oz. fresh yeast
1/2 cup lukewarm water
1 tsp. sea salt
4 eggs
1/2 cup light tasting olive oil
5-3/4 cups white whole wheat flour
1/4 cup vital wheat gluten

In a large bowl dissolve yeast in water. Combine all ingredients and knead well until smooth. This can be done with a heavy duty mixer. Let rise in a warm place until doubled in size, about one hour. Be sure to cover the dough well so it doesn't dry out. Punch down and let rise again. Shape dough into bagels by tearing off pieces, rolling into a rope and turning the rope into a bagel shape.

Preheat oven to 400 degrees. Drop bagels into boiling salted water and boil for 3 minutes. Remove from water. Place on an ungreased cookie sheet and bake for 15-18 minutes, until golden brown.

SOFT PRETZELS

2 cups white whole wheat flour
3 Tbsp. vital wheat gluten
1 Tbsp. light tasting olive oil
1 Tbsp. active dry yeast
3/4 cup lukewarm apple juice
1 egg
Kosher salt

Combine 1 cup flour with oil, yeast and apple juice in the bowl of a heavy duty mixer (or if doing this by hand, use a large bowl). Beat for 3 minutes. Add the remaining flour and vital wheat gluten and knead for 10 minutes until the dough is smooth and elastic.

If the dough is too sticky, add more flour. Tear off pieces of dough and roll into a long rope. Twist into a pretzel shape by forming a loop with the rope and crossing one end over the other. Twist the top once and bend the twist down into the circle to form that 3 ringed pretzel shape. Place pretzels on a lightly greased baking sheet and let them rise for 30 minutes. Preheat oven to 450 degrees. Beat the egg and brush the pretzels with the egg wash. Sprinkle with kosher salt and bake for 15 minutes until golden brown.

ONION BREAD

1 cup lukewarm water
1 package dry yeast
1 tsp. sea salt
3 cups white whole wheat flour
4-1/2 Tbsp. vital wheat gluten
1/4 cup light tasting olive oil
1 cup chopped onion
2 tsp. paprika
1/2 tsp. sea salt - optional

Pour warm water into the bowl of a heavy duty mixer (or if doing this by hand, a large bowl). Sprinkle yeast over water and stir until dissolved. Add 2 cups of the flour and mix until well blended. Add additional flour and the vital wheat gluten and 1 tsp. salt to make a stiff dough. Knead until smooth and elastic.

Place in a well oiled bowl and turn to coat all sides with oil. Let rise until doubled in size, about one hour. Punch the dough down and divide into half. Cover and let rest for 5 minutes.

Place into two greased 9" cake pans. Brush with oil and sprinkle with onion, pressing onion into the dough with fingertips. Let rise uncovered for 45 minutes. Preheat oven to 450 degrees. Sprinkle tops with paprika and 1/2 tsp. sea salt. Bake for 20-25 minutes. Cool on wire racks.

Vital wheat gluten helps 100% whole grain breads to rise and have a lighter, fluffier texture.

CORN BREAD

1 cup milk
1/4 cup butter, melted
1 egg
1-1/4 cups cornmeal
1 cup whole wheat pastry flour
1/2 cup applesauce
1 Tbsp. baking powder
1/2 tsp. salt

Beat milk, butter and egg with fork. Stir in remaining ingredients all at once until combined. Do not over mix. Pour batter into an 8" square pan. Bake at 400 degrees for 20-25 minutes until golden brown and a toothpick inserted in center comes out clean.

You can substitute 1/3 cup of brown rice flour and 2/3 cup of oat flour for the wheat flour

APPETIZERS

SPINACH DIP

1 package frozen spinach, thawed and drained
1/2 cup finely chopped onion
1/2 cup finely chopped parsley
2 cups mayonnaise
1/2 tsp. lemon juice
1/2 tsp. sea salt
1/2 tsp. pepper

Mix well. Serve with fresh cut-up vegetables and whole grain crackers.

CHUMUS

2 cans of chickpeas (garbanzo beans), drained OR
      4 cups of cooked chickpeas
8 oz. tahini (sesame butter – mixed according to
      package directions)
1/2 cup lemon juice
2 cloves garlic, crushed
1/2 tsp. cumin
1/2 tsp. salt
1/8 tsp. pepper
1 Tbsp. light tasting olive oil (optional)
2 tsp. paprika (garnish)
2 tsp. chopped parsley (garnish)

Blend all ingredients in a blender or food processor, except oil and garnishes. Place in serving dish and drizzle oil on top. Sprinkle with paprika and parsley. Serve with vegetables, whole grain crackers and whole grain pita.

Variation: you can add 1/4 cup of cooked chickpeas to the blended mixture before drizzling the oil and topping with the garnishes

BOUREKAS

1/2 lb butter or Earth Balance margarine (do not soften)
2-1/4 cups whole wheat pastry flour
2 Tbsp. vinegar
1 egg yolk
1/2 cup ice water
Whole wheat pastry flour for dusting

Mix the butter and 1/2 cup flour in a food processor or heavy duty mixer until smooth. Using the machine, knead very well and then shape into a ball. Cover and refrigerate it. Combine 1-3/4 cups flour, vinegar, egg yolk and ice water. Keep mixing until well combined and smooth. Form into a ball. Dust pastry board or cloth with flour and roll out the dough. Cut the chilled butter dough into thin slices. Place the thin slices over the rolled out dough. Fold the left side of the dough towards the center and the right side of the dough towards the center (so it is essentially in thirds) and then roll out. Repeat the folding and rolling process three times. Fold it again and wrap in wax paper. Refrigerate overnight. The next day, repeat the folding and rolling process another two times, making sure your pastry board or cloth is well dusted with flour. Roll out 1/8" thick and fill.

CHEESE FILLING:
1-8 oz. package cream cheese
1-8 oz. package farmers cheese
2 egg yolks
1/2 tsp. salt
1/8 tsp. pepper

Mix ingredients well. Cut 2" to 6" squares and fill with cheese filling, folding the dough over the filling and sealing the edges, forming a triangle. Brush the filled dough with egg yolk and sprinkle with sesame seeds. Bake in 400 degree oven for 25 minutes or until golden brown.

POTATO FILLING:
6 white potatoes – unpeeled
3 medium onions, sliced
1/2 cup light tasting olive oil
2 tsp. sea salt and 1/8 tsp. pepper

Cut potatoes into quarters. Boil in water until tender and drain. Sauté sliced onions in oil until caramelized. Using the "S" blade of a food processor, process potatoes, onions and seasonings until smooth. Cut dough into 4" to 6" rectangles and fill with potato filling, folding the dough over the filling and sealing the edges. Brush the filled dough with egg yolk and sprinkle with sesame seeds. Bake in 400 degree oven for 25 minutes or until golden brown.

STUFFED BABY SQUASH

15 baby zucchini or yellow squash (little 4 " size)
16 oz. tomato sauce
6 oz. tomato paste
1/2 lb ground beef
1/2 lb ground turkey
2 Tbsp. light tasting olive oil
3 medium onions, diced
1 Tbsp. cumin
1/2 tsp. sea salt
1/8 tsp. pepper
1/2 cup fresh parsley, chopped

Sauté onion in oil over medium-high heat until light brown. Add meat and stir constantly until browned. Add parsley, cumin, salt and pepper and 3 Tbsp. tomato paste. Cover and cook over medium heat for 30 minutes. Meanwhile, clean squash. Cut off the caps of the squash (the end) and core squash with an apple corer, so you are making a tube, where you can put the stuffing (see note). Stuff the squash with the meat mixture.

Arrange in a large greased roasting pan. Mix together the tomato sauce and remaining paste and pour over the squash. Bake at 350 for 40 minutes.

If you do not have an apple corer, you can also make these into little boats. You do this by cutting the squash in half and scooping out the middle to make room for the meat mixture. Stuff the meat mixture into the little scooped out area and proceed as above.
You can lower the fat content by using only ground turkey. If you have trouble locating baby squash, you can also use whole squash, cut into pieces and proceed as above.

MOCK CHOPPED LIVER

3 large onions, coarsely chopped
3 Tbsp. light tasting olive oil
1 lb. walnuts
6 hard boiled eggs
2 Tbsp. mayonnaise
1/2 tsp. salt
1/8 tsp. pepper

Sauté onions in oil until caramelized. Mix all ingredients together in a food processor until smooth. Chill and serve with whole grain crackers or whole grain bread.

STUFFED MUSHROOMS

Ryvita is a whole rye cracker that you can use to make dried bread crumbs. Just place a few crackers in your food processor and process them until they are completely ground up.

24 large mushrooms
1 Tbsp. light tasting olive oil
1/2 cup chicken broth or vegetable broth
2 Tbsp. light tasting olive oil
3 Tbsp. green onions, chopped
1 tsp. granulated garlic powder
1/2 tsp. salt
1/8 tsp. pepper
3 Tbsp. whole grain bread crumbs or Ryvita crumbs
2 Tbsp. parsley, chopped

Wash mushrooms thoroughly and gently. Carefully separate the stems from the caps. Sauté mushroom caps in combination of oil and broth for about 3 minutes. Remove caps and place into a baking dish. Chop the mushroom stems into small cubes and fry in oil with green onions. Add seasonings. Cook, stirring occasionally for 5 minutes. Add bread crumbs and parsley. Fill mushroom caps with the breadcrumb mixture. Bake in a 375 oven for 8 minutes.

FALAFEL

1 lb dry chick peas (garbanzo beans)
2 Tbsp. baking soda
water to cover
1/4 cup chopped parsley
3 slices whole grain bread, soaked & drained
4 cloves garlic, crushed
2 tsp. cumin
1 tsp. turmeric (optional)
vegetable oil for frying

Cover chickpeas with water and baking soda. Soak overnight. Drain chickpeas. In a food processor, process the chickpeas with bread, parsley and garlic. Add seasonings and mix. Let stand for 30 minutes. Heat oil in a large deep skillet or deep fryer at 350 degrees. Form the mixture into balls and drop into the hot oil and fry on both sides until golden brown. Drain on paper towels.

CHICKEN FINGERS

4 chicken breasts, boneless and skinless
2 eggs
1/4 cup water
3/4 cup whole wheat pastry flour or oat flour
1 tsp. granulated garlic
1/2 tsp. salt
1/8 tsp. pepper
vegetable oil for frying

Cut chicken into small finger sized pieces. Season flour with salt and pepper. Beat eggs with water. Dip chicken pieces into flour and then into egg. Fry until golden brown. Serve with spicy sauce.

SPICY SAUCE:
1/2 cup sugar-free ketchup
1/2 cup mustard
2 tsp. white horseradish
1 Tbsp. apple juice

Mix well.

MINI CORN DOGS

1 pkg. beef, chicken or tofu hot dogs – no sugar & no nitrates
1 cup corn meal
1 cup whole wheat pastry flour
2 tsp. baking soda
1 tsp. salt and 1/4 tsp. pepper
1 tsp. onion powder
1 cup water
2 eggs
1/4 cup whole wheat pastry flour for dusting
vegetable oil for frying

If the batter gets too thick, you can thin it down with a little more water, adding water by the tablespoon until it is the right consistency.

Mix corn meal, flour and seasonings together. Add eggs and water, mixing until mixture is smooth and a thick consistency. Place the corndog mixture into a small cup (you will need to do this in batches). Cut each hot dog into 4-6 pieces, depending on how large you want them. Place hot dog pieces in a large Ziploc bag and add 1/4 cup flour. Close the bag and shake well to coat each piece in flour. To coat the hot dogs with the cornmeal mixture, take a toothpick and insert it into the end of the hotdog piece. Dip each hot dog into the batter in the small cup, twirling several times to coat well. Fry in oil until crisp and golden brown on each side. These are great dipped in mustard!

MAHOGANY CHICKEN WINGS

15 chicken wings (3 lbs)
1/2 cup soy sauce
1/2 cup apple butter
1/4 cup all fruit apricot spread (no sweetener added)
2 Tbsp. sugar free ketchup
2 tsp. chili powder
1 tsp. ground ginger
2 cloves garlic, finely chopped

Cut each chicken wing at joints to make 3 pieces. Discard tip. Cut off excess skin and discard. Place chicken in shallow glass or plastic bowl. Mix remaining ingredients; pour over chicken. Cover and refrigerate 1 hour, turning occasionally.

Heat oven to 375 degrees. Line broiler pan with foil.

Remove chicken from marinade; reserve marinade. Place chicken in a single layer on a rack in foil-lined broiler pan; brush with marinade.

Bake 30 minutes; turn. Bake about 20 minutes longer, brushing occasionally with marinade, until deep brown and juice of chicken is no longer pink when centers of thickest part are cut. Discard any remaining marinade.

SOUPS

SPLIT PEA & BARLEY SOUP

10 cups water
1 cup split peas
1 cup barley
2 onions, chopped
4 carrots, chopped
1 sweet potato, cubed
2 stalks celery, chopped
2-4 cloves garlic,(I like to use 4 cloves as I am a big
     garlic lover), minced
4 zucchini, chopped
2 Tbsp. salt (or to your taste)
Optional: for a fleishig (meat) soup, add some
meat bones or turkey necks

Put all ingredients in a large pot. Bring to boil over
medium-high heat. Simmer over very low heat for at least
two hours, stirring occasionally. The longer you cook it, the
better it is. Just be careful not to let the barley and split peas
burn on the bottom of the pot!

CHICKEN BROTH

3 lb chicken, skinned and defatted
1 lb chicken bones or necks
2 large carrots
1 large onion
4 cloves garlic
1 parsnip
3 stalks celery
1 bunch parsley
1 bunch dill
1 sweet potato, peeled

Rinse chicken parts and put into a large stock pot. Add
bones. Cover chicken and bones with water, making sure
that it is not more than 1 inch over the chicken and bones.
Boil chicken and bones. When it boils, skim the pot. When
clean, add all the vegetables and bring back to a boil. Lower
heat and simmer for at least 3 hours. Strain broth. Chill soup
and skim all the fat off before reheating and serving

*I find the Landau's
boil-n-bags to be
very helpful in
straining, I put the
bones in one bag
and the vegetables
(except carrots) in
another. I discard
those bags and
just remove the
chicken and
carrots.*

MINESTRONE SOUP

2 quarts water
1 Tbsp. salt
3 Tbsp. light tasting olive oil
2 onions, diced
3 cloves garlic, crushed
3 Tbsp. tomato paste
1 can peeled tomatoes (14 oz. can)
1/2 cup diced carrots
1/2 cup diced celery
1 tsp. parsley
1 cup cut green beans, frozen
1 cup peas, frozen
1 cup lima beans, frozen
1/2 cup diced zucchini
1/2 cup spinach, frozen or wilted fresh
1/2 cup brown rice pasta

Combine water, salt, oil, onion, garlic, tomato paste and peeled tomatoes in a large pot. Bring to a boil and simmer for 10 – 15 minutes. Add carrots, celery and parsley and continue simmering for 20 minutes. Add the rest of the ingredients except the brown rice pasta and continuing simmering until all the vegetables are tender, about one hour. Add brown rice pasta and cook on high heat for 3 minutes, stir well and cover the pot. Remove from heat and let it stand for 20 minutes. Stir well and serve.

TOMATO & RICE SOUP

1 lb. flanken (a cut of beef taken from the short ribs)
1 (46 oz.) can of tomato juice
1 empty can (46 oz.) of water
1 onion, diced
4 carrots, sliced
1 stalk celery, diced
2 tsp. sea salt
1/8 tsp. black pepper
1/2 cup uncooked brown rice

Brown flanken in a large pot. Add tomato juice and water and bring to a boil. Add all the remaining ingredients, except rice. Reduce heat and simmer for 1 hour. Add rice and cook until rice is tender, about 45 minutes.

SUPER SPEEDY VEGETABLE SOUP

1 large Imagine Soup – any flavor
1-16oz. package frozen mixed vegetables
1 onion, chopped
3 cloves garlic, minced
1/2 cup lentils
1 zucchini, chopped
1 tsp. sea salt, to taste
water, as needed

Sauté onion and garlic until translucent. Add zucchini, lentils and frozen vegetables and sauté for 4 minutes. Add the Imagine soup and sea salt and stir well. Bring to a boil. Lower heat to a simmer and cook for 2 hours. If you like a thinner soup, add some water to the pot.

CABBAGE SOUP

2 Tbsp. light tasting olive oil
1 large Spanish onion, chopped
1 small cabbage OR
        1-16 oz. package shredded cabbage
1 (46 oz.) can no sugar added tomato juice
2 cups water
1/2 cup apple juice
1 Tbsp. sea salt
2 cloves garlic, crushed

Heat oil in large pot. Add onion and sauté until translucent. Add cabbage and sauté until cabbage is lightly browned. Add tomato juice, water and apple juice. Add salt and garlic. Bring to a boil and simmer for 1-1/2 hours.

Optional: can use one large turkey neck for a meat based and more flavorful soup.

VEGETARIAN CHILI 〗

2 Tbsp. light tasting olive oil
1 large onion, diced
1 large red pepper, diced
2 cups textured vegetable protein crumbles (TVP)
1 (15.5 oz.) can kidney beans, NOT drained
1 (14.5 oz.) can diced tomatoes – no sugar added,
    NOT drained
1 (15 oz.) can tomato sauce – no sugar added
1 tsp. chili powder
1/2 tsp. cumin
1 tsp. paprika
2 Tbsp. crushed garlic

TVP is a soy protein that is dried and when rehydrated tastes like meat. You can find this protein source in your local health food store.

Sauté onion and pepper in oil until soft. Add textured vegetable protein crumbles, beans, diced tomatoes and tomato sauce. Mix. Add spices and mix. Simmer for 15 minutes.

BORSCHT

8 beets
2 quarts water
1 lemon, juiced
1 Tbsp. sea salt
4 eggs
2 tsp. salt
1 Tbsp. cold water

Scrub beets well. Cook unpeeled beets in water until soft. When cooled enough to handle, peel and grate the beets. Add lemon juice and salt and then return beets to water. Beat eggs with 2 tsp. salt and 1 Tbsp. cold water. Add one ladle of hot borscht to beaten eggs and very quickly beat together, then very quickly add the egg mixture to the pot of borscht and quickly mix together. Do not boil the borscht. Heat carefully. For a dairy meal, you can add some sour cream as a garnish. If you want a meat borscht, add some meat bones to the beets before cooking

CREAM OF ASPARAGUS SOUP

3 Tbsp. light tasting olive oil
3 Tbsp. whole wheat or brown rice flour
1-1/2 quarts of chicken broth
1 Tbsp. crushed garlic
1 package of frozen cut up asparagus (16 oz.)

Make a roux by heating the oil in a soup pot and then adding the flour, mixing well. Slowly add the broth, bit by bit, stirring well after each addition to avoid lumps. Add the garlic and bring to a boil. Add the asparagus and cook for 1/2 hour. Blend with a hand blender or regular blender to make a smooth soup.

BEAN & POTATO CHOWDER

2 Tbsp. light tasting olive oil
1 cup chopped onion
1/2 cup chopped celery
1/2 cup chopped yellow bell pepper
1/4 cup chopped red bell pepper
1 garlic clover, minced
2-1/4 cups water
2 cups (1/2 inch) cubed potato, unpeeled
2 cups canned diced tomatoes and green chilies,
    undrained
1 cup canned chickpeas (garbanzo beans), rinsed
    and drained
1 tsp. ground cumin
1/8 tsp. black pepper
2-1/2 cups chicken broth or beef broth
1 (16 oz.) can kidney beans, rinsed and drained
1 (16 oz.) can navy beans, rinsed and drained
1 lb. leftover cooked chicken, cubed

Heat oil in a Dutch oven over medium-high heat. Add the onion, celery, bell peppers and garlic; sauté 5 minutes or until crisp-tender.

Add water and the rest of the ingredients and bring to a boil. Reduce heat, and simmer 30 minutes, stirring occasionally.

WHOLE WHEAT MATZO BALLS 🌾

For the best tasting matzo balls, I drop them into extra chicken broth because I think it gives them a better flavor than plain salt water.

2 eggs
2 Tbsp. light tasting olive oil
1/4 cup very fizzy seltzer (soda water)
1/2 tsp. salt
1/2 tsp. garlic powder
1/2 cup whole wheat matzo meal
    (see miscellaneous section)
1-1/2 quarts boiling water with 1 tsp. salt added

Beat eggs well, add oil, seltzer, salt, and garlic. Beat thoroughly. Slowly add matzo meal. Refrigerate for 20 minutes. Form matzo balls with wet hands, you may have to keep wetting your hands. Drop balls into boiling salted water.

SALADS & DRESSINGS

VINAIGRETTE

1/4 cup red-wine vinegar
1/2 cup olive oil
3 Tbsp. Dijon mustard
3 Tbsp. chopped onions
1-2 cloves garlic, pressed
2 Tbsp. dill (fresh or dried)
dash of sea salt
freshly ground pepper, to taste

Mix all ingredients together in a blender.

ROASTED GARLIC DRESSING

1/2 cup brown rice vinegar
1 cup olive oil
2 tsp. sea salt
1 head of garlic, roasted

To roast garlic: peel garlic, place on a large piece of foil and drizzle with olive oil. Fold corners of foil to make a packet. Roast at 400 degrees for 1/2 hour. Open packet and roast for another 10 minutes. Let cool before adding to the dressing ingredients. Puree all ingredients in a blender or food processor. Best if you let it sit for 24 hours before serving.

BALSAMIC MUSTARD DRESSING

1/2 cup balsamic vinegar
1 cup olive oil
2 tsp. sea salt
4 cloves garlic, crushed
2 tsp. Dijon mustard

Mix all ingredients together.

THOUSAND ISLAND DRESSING

1 cup mayonnaise
2 Tbsp. regular pickle relish (not sweet)
4 Tbsp. sugar free ketchup
1 tsp. onion, minced
1 Tbsp. garlic, crushed
1 hard boiled egg

Blend all ingredients in a blender.

GARLIC DRESSING

1/2 cup mayonnaise
1 Tbsp. garlic, crushed
1 Tbsp. balsamic vinegar
3 Tbsp. apple juice

Mix well.

For Dairy dressings, see dairy section.

SPINACH SALAD

1-16 oz. package of fresh spinach
1 red onion
1 quart package of mushrooms
Poppy Seed Dressing (recipe next page)

Wash and check spinach very thoroughly. Dry spinach leaves well. Slice onion into rings, separate rings. Check mushrooms, slice very thinly. Toss onions and mushrooms with spinach.

POPPY SEED DRESSING

1/4 cup balsamic vinegar
1/2 cup light tasting olive oil
3 Tbsp. chopped onions
1-2 cloves garlic, pressed
3 Tbsp. apple juice
3 Tbsp. poppy seeds
dash of sea salt

If you are concerned about eating spinach, you can substitute the spinach with any other type of dark leafy green.

Blend all ingredients in a blender until smooth.

EASY MARINATED BEAN SALAD

2/3 cup brown rice vinegar
1/4 cup water
1/2 tsp. sea salt
3 cloves garlic crushed
1/4 cup apple juice
I can kidney beans or 2 cups cooked
I can green beans or 2 cups cooked
I can wax beans (yellow beans) or 2 cups cooked
I can chickpeas (garbanzo beans) or 2 cups
     cooked
2 medium red onions sliced very thinly

Do not substitute the brown rice vinegar for another type of vinegar as the slight sweetness of the brown rice vinegar adds the right touch to this delicious salad.

Drain and rinse canned beans very well. Boil vinegar, water, salt, garlic and apple juice and cook for approximately 2 minutes. Let cool. Add remaining ingredients to vinegar mixture. Marinate in refrigerator at least one day before serving.

TOMATO SALAD

8 large hothouse tomatoes
1 large or 2 small red onions
2 stalks scallions
1 Tbsp. sea salt
1 Tbsp. fresh lemon juice
2 Tbsp. light tasting olive oil
1 Tbsp. freshly crushed garlic

Thinly slice tomatoes and red onions. Wash and check scallions and then dice. Mix all ingredients together and let marinate for 24 hours before serving.

PINEAPPLE COLESLAW

You can freeze the extra pineapple in freezer bags for a later use. If you are sensitive to pineapple, you can also decrease the amount of the pineapple to 1/4 cup.

1-16 oz. package coleslaw mix
2 extra carrots, grated
1/2 cup crushed pineapple in its own juice
1/2 cup mayonnaise

Mix all ingredients together. Let marinate for 4 hours before serving. This salad should be eaten within 2 days.

PURPLE CABBAGE SALAD

1 package red cabbage (like a coleslaw)
1 Vidalia onion, thinly sliced
1/2 fresh lemon, squeezed
1/2 cup mayonnaise

Mix all ingredients together. Let marinate overnight.

CARROT SALAD

6 carrots, peeled
2 apples, unpeeled
1/2 cup mayonnaise
2 Tbsp. lemon juice
1 tsp. salt
1/2 cup walnuts, chopped

Finely grate carrots. Add thickly grated unpeeled apples. Add mayonnaise, lemon juice and salt. Mix well. Toss with walnuts right before serving. If you are leaving any portions for leftovers, do not add the walnuts until before serving as they get quite soggy.

SPINACH BEAN SPROUT SALAD

8 oz. fresh bean sprouts
2 tsp. vinegar (any flavor you like – **NOT** white)
4 Tbsp. light tasting olive oil
1/2 tsp. salt
1/2 tsp. black pepper
3 Tbsp. soy sauce
1 clove fresh garlic, crushed
1 package prechecked and washed spinach
1 (5 oz.) can sliced water chestnuts, drained
2 Tbsp. toasted sesame seeds
1 tsp. paprika

Toast sesame seeds in a dry frying pan over high heat until golden brown, stirring often.

Place bean sprouts in a colander and pour boiling water over them. Drain well. Place the sprouts in a medium bowl. Mix the vinegar, oil, salt, pepper, soy sauce and garlic and then pour over the warm bean sprouts. Marinate for at least 6 hours, stirring occasionally. Tear spinach into bite sized pieces. Combine with water chestnuts, sesame seeds and paprika. Add bean sprout mixture and gently toss to coat the spinach. Serve immediately.

MIXED VEGETABLE SALAD

2 large tomatoes, diced
1 large cucumber, diced
1 bunch radishes, sliced
1 bunch scallions, chopped
1 large pickle, diced
1 large orange pepper, diced
1/4 cup light tasting olive oil
1/4 cup chopped parsley
2 Tbsp. lemon juice
2 Tbsp. pickle juice
2 garlic cloves, crushed
salt and pepper to taste

Combine vegetables, olive oil and parsley. Mix remaining ingredients together and then pour over the vegetable mixture. You can serve this immediately or let it marinate in the refrigerator for a few hours before serving.

RED POTATO SALAD

9 small red potatoes
1 Spanish onion
1/4 cup chopped parsley
1 clove garlic, crushed
3 Tbsp. white wine vinegar
4 Tbsp. light tasting olive oil
sea salt, to taste
black pepper, to taste

Scrub potatoes well and boil until tender. Cut boiled potatoes into thin slices. Slice onion into thin rings. In a shallow bowl, alternate layers of potatoes and onions. Sprinkle each layer with parsley, salt and pepper. Combine vinegar and oil and pour over the layers. Refrigerate overnight, turning mixture at least once while it is marinating

ASPARAGUS VINAIGRETTE

1-1/2 lb. asparagus, cooked
1/3 cup light tasting olive oil
1/4 cup fresh lemon juice
1/8 tsp. pepper
1 garlic clove, crushed
1/8 tsp. dry mustard
1/8 tsp. sea salt
1 egg yolk, hard boiled and chopped
Lettuce leaves

Combine olive oil, lemon juice, pepper, garlic, mustard and salt. Marinate asparagus spears in dressing for at least 2 hours. Drain and arrange on lettuce leaves. Sprinkle with the chopped egg yolk.

COLORFUL PASTA SALAD

32 oz. whole wheat or brown rice spiral pasta
1 red pepper, diced
1 yellow pepper, diced
1 orange pepper, diced
1 medium red onion, diced
4 scallions, minced
1/2 cup light tasting olive oil
1/4 cup balsamic vinegar
salt and pepper, to taste

Cook pasta according to package directions. Drain and cool. Mix pasta with vegetables, oil, vinegar and seasonings. Chill overnight. Mix well before serving chilled

COLD GREEN BEAN SALAD

1 lb. green beans
1 clove garlic, crushed
1/4 tsp. sea salt
4 Tbsp. wine vinegar
1/2 tsp. dry mustard
1/2 tsp. Dijon mustard
1/8 tsp. black pepper
1/8 tsp. oregano
1/8 tsp. basil
1/8 tsp. parsley
3/4 cup light tasting olive oil
1/4 cup sliced olives (optional)
1/2 cup slivered almonds

Cook green beans in salted water until crisp tender, about 5 minutes. Drain and cool in ice water. Mix all ingredients except olives and almonds and pour over the green beans. Refrigerate for at least 2 hours. Add the olives and almonds right before serving.

VEGETABLES & SIDES

TZIMMES

1 lb baby carrots
6 sweet potatoes
1/4 cup orange juice
1 cup water
1/2 cup unsweetened apple sauce
1/2 tsp. salt
1/2 tsp. cinnamon
2 Tbsp. light tasting olive oil

Combine all ingredients and cook in a covered pot over low heat until tender, about 45 minutes.

MAPLE ORANGE GLAZED CARROTS
(perfect for Rosh Hashana!)

12 medium carrots
2 Tbsp. light tasting olive oil
2 Tbsp. orange juice
grated zest from one small orange
1 tsp. sea salt
2 tsp. nutmeg
2 Tbsp. apple juice concentrate
1 Tbsp. alcohol-free sugar-free maple extract

When grating citrus fruits for zest, be sure to only use the colored parts, avoiding the bitter white part.

Peel the carrots and then slice into 1/4" pieces. Place carrots in a covered vegetable steamer over boiling water for 10 minutes or until they are tender. Remove from heat and set aside. Heat the oil in a large saucepan. Add orange juice, orange zest, steamed carrots, salt, nutmeg and apple juice concentrate. Stir to coat and cook until heated through. Remove from heat and add maple extract, mixing well. Serve immediately.

PECAN TOPPED YAMS

4 medium Jewel or Garnet yams
2 Tbsp. light tasting olive oil
1/4 cup orange juice, optional
1 cup chopped pecans
1 Tbsp. alcohol-free maple extract
1 Tbsp. orange or apple juice concentrate
2 tsp. cinnamon
pinch of sea salt

Preheat oven to 400°F. Bake yams for about one hour, or until soft. The skins should peel off easily when they are still warm. Mash yams well and mix with oil and juice. Place yams in a 8" square glass baking dish. Spread evenly and flatten.

Toss pecans with maple extract, juice concentrate, cinnamon and a pinch of salt. Spread evenly over the top of the yams. Bake until pecans are toasted and the yams are hot and bubbly (start checking after 10 minutes).

STUFFED ACORN SQUASH

2 acorn squash, halved, seeds and strings removed
2 cups water
3/4 cup walnuts, chopped
1/2 cup red apples with peel on, chopped
1 Tbsp. cinnamon
2 Tbsp. light tasting olive oil

Place squash halves cut sides down on cutting board. Trim 1/4 inch from the rounded top of each squash so that they will stand level when filled. Arrange squash, hollow sides down, in oblong microwave safe baking dish and add the water. Cover dish with plastic wrap, leaving one corner open for vent. Microwave on high until almost cooked through, about 10-12 minutes. Meanwhile, combine nuts, apples, cinnamon and oil. Pour water from baking dish and turn squash over. Divide nut mixture evenly among squash halves. Microwave on high, covered and vented, about 4 minutes. Serve warm.

CABBAGE WITH CARAWAY

1 small cabbage, shredded OR
    1 package shredded cabbage
1 cup water
1/2 tsp. marjoram
1 tsp. salt
3 Tbsp. light tasting olive oil
1 tsp. caraway seeds

Cook cabbage with water and seasonings until tender, but still crisp. Drain. Add oil and top with caraway seeds.

CABBAGE AND RICE

1 large Spanish onion, chopped
2 cloves garlic, crushed
1 small cabbage, shredded or 1 package shredded
    cabbage
3 Tbsp. light tasting olive oil
2 cups brown rice, cooked and room temperature
1 cup slivered, roasted almonds

Sauté onion, garlic and cabbage in oil until tender, stirring often to prevent burning. Mix cabbage with cooked brown rice. Sprinkle almonds on top and serve immediately.

If you cannot locate the mushroom soup, you may substitute by making a roux: 2 Tbsp. oil and 2 Tbsp. flour and slowly add 1-1/4 cups soy milk. Cook it until it is thick and creamy. Add 1/2 cup finely chopped cooked mushrooms, 1 Tbsp. minced garlic and 1 Tbsp. minced onion. Salt to taste.

GREEN BEAN CASSEROLE

2 Tbsp. light tasting olive oil
1 large Spanish onion, chopped
1-1/4 cups Imagine Portobello Mushroom Soup
1 lb. fresh green beans, lightly steamed
1/2 cup sliced almonds, optional

Sauté onion in oil until golden brown in color. Add the mushroom soup and cook until thickened. Add the green beans and pour into an oiled 2 quart casserole dish. Bake for 1 hour at 350 degrees. If using almonds, add them to the top of the casserole during the last 10 minutes.

FOUR COLOR GREEN BEANS

1 lb fresh string beans
1 large red pepper
1 large orange pepper
1 large yellow pepper
2 large garlic cloves, crushed
2 Tbsp. light tasting olive oil
salt to taste

Prepare green beans by snapping off the ends and rinsing well. Prepare peppers by discarding seeds and membranes and cutting into strips, julienne style. In a large frying pan, warm oil over medium heat. Add vegetables, garlic and salt. Stir well. Cover and cook on low until vegetables are tender, stirring occasionally, about 30 minutes.

RATATOUILLE

1 onion, diced
1/4 cup light tasting olive oil
1 eggplant, peeled and sliced
2 zucchini, sliced
1 green pepper, diced
2 tomatoes, sliced
1/2 tsp. basil
2 cloves garlic, crushed
1/2 tsp. oregano
1/8 tsp. black pepper
1 tsp. sea salt (optional)

Sauté onion in oil for 4 minutes, add the remaining
ingredients, mixing well. Sauté over medium-low heat until
all the vegetables are tender, about 30-40 minutes.

BROCCOLI WITH MUSTARD SAUCE

1 Tbsp. light tasting olive oil
1 Tbsp. apple juice
1 Tbsp. Dijon or spicy brown mustard
1 Tbsp. water
1 Tbsp. light tasting olive oil
1 lb. broccoli
3 Tbsp. water

Mix oil, apple juice, mustard and water together. Set aside.
Heat oil in a large skillet over medium-high heat. Add
broccoli and cook for about 1 minute. Add water and cover.
Cook for 3 minutes or until broccoli is crisp-tender. Add
mustard mixture and toss, cooking for 1 more minute.

SUMMER SQUASH & MUSHROOMS

You can substitute zucchini for the yellow squash or even use a pound of each kind for a really colorful vegetable dish.

1/4 cup light tasting olive oil
1 cup sliced onions
1/4 lb. fresh mushrooms, sliced
2 lb. yellow squash, sliced
1-1/2 tsp. sea salt
1/2 tsp. oregano leaves
1/8 tsp. black pepper
1/4 cup water
parsley for garnish, if desired

In large skillet, sauté onion in oil until golden. Add sliced mushrooms. Add squash, spices and water. Cook over medium heat, covered for about 15 minutes or until squash is tender. Make sure to stir the ingredients a few times while it is cooking. You may sprinkle the vegetables with parsley right before serving.

ROASTED VEGETABLES

2 medium zucchini, cut into chunks, unpeeled
2 medium yellow squash, cut into chunks, unpeeled
1 medium eggplant, cut into chunks, unpeeled
1 lb. small button mushrooms
1 red bell pepper, cut into chunks
1 orange bell pepper, cut into chunks
1 large onion, cut into 8 wedges,
    and separate each layer
4 garlic cloves, cut in half
1/4 cup fresh basil, chopped
1 tsp. oregano
1/2 tsp. sea salt
1/4 tsp. black pepper
3 Tbsp. light tasting olive oil
2 Tbsp. apple cider vinegar

Preheat oven to 350 degrees. Place all the vegetables in a roasting pan. Sprinkle with basil and spices. Mix oil and vinegar together and pour oven the vegetables. Bake uncovered for 45 minutes or until vegetables are tender

VEGETABLE LATKES (PANCAKES)

1 cup chopped onion
2 cloves garlic, crushed
1/4 cup chopped red bell pepper
1/4 cup chopped green pepper
1-1/2 cups grated carrots
1/4 cup chopped celery
1-10 oz. package of frozen spinach
3 Tbsp. light tasting olive oil
1/8 tsp. pepper
3 eggs, beaten
3/4 cup whole wheat matzo meal or finely ground
    rye cracker crumbs
1-1/2 tsp. sea salt
light tasting olive oil for frying

Sauté onion, garlic, red and green peppers, carrots and celery for 10 minutes. Cook and drain spinach. Combine all vegetables. Add eggs and seasonings and mix well. Add matzo meal and combine well. Refrigerate for 15 minutes. Form mixture into patties and fry in oil until browned on each side.

GREEN BEAN ALMONDINE

1 lb. fresh string beans
2 large garlic cloves, crushed
2 Tbsp. light tasting olive oil
salt to taste
1/2 cup sliced almonds, toasted

To toast almonds, place them in a dry frying pan over medium heat until golden brown, stirring often. Remove from heat and let cool.

Prepare green beans by snapping off the ends and rinsing well. Heat oil in frying pan and add green beans and garlic. Steam in pan over low heat until tender. Add salt (if desired) and almonds and toss. Serve immediately.

POTATO KNISHES 🌾

DOUGH:
2 cups whole wheat pastry flour
2 tsp. baking powder
1 tsp. salt
1/4 cup Earth Balance margarine
3/4 cup apple juice
1 egg, beaten to glaze

FILLING:
6 medium white potatoes, scrubbed
    and unpeeled
1/4 cup light tasting olive oil
2 large onions, minced
2 cloves garlic, crushed
1 Tbsp. sea salt
1-1/2 tsp. black pepper
2 eggs, beaten

In a large bowl mix flour with baking powder and salt. Cut in margarine with a pastry blender or 2 forks until the dough resembles coarse crumbs. Add 1/2 cup of apple juice and mix. Add the rest of the juice, 1 tablespoon at a time until the dough can be gathered together into a ball and has a moist, smooth consistency (you may not need all the juice or you may need even more, use your judgment). Knead for 1 minute. Cover and refrigerate 30 minutes.

Boil potatoes in salted water. Cook until tender. While still warm, mash the potatoes well. Heat the oil in a skillet and sauté the onions until golden. Add garlic and sauté 1-2 minutes or until soft. Add onions and garlic with oil to mashed potatoes. Add seasonings and eggs. Preheat oven to 350 degrees.

Divide the dough in half. Roll each half into a 10" x 15" rectangle. Place half the filling 1" up from the bottom and 1" from either edge. Roll filled dough over and tuck the ends under. Place on a greased cookie sheet. Brush with egg glaze and cut through the dough at 2" intervals. Repeat with the second half. Bake 35- 40 minutes or until golden brown.

This dish is worth all the extra preparation and your family will love it. They won't even notice that the potatoes have the peel on and their bodies will love the extra nutrition and fiber that the peel provides. For a really fancy dish, you can use the mushroom sauce substitution mentioned in the notes for the green bean casserole.

SQUASH WITH TOMATO SAUCE

1 lb. green squash
1 lb. yellow squash
1 large spanish onion
2 Tbsp. light tasting olive oil
2 cloves garlic, crushed
2 Tbsp. sugar free ketchup
I medium can of tomato sauce
salt to taste

Cut squash into half-moon shapes. Chop onion. In a large saucepan, heat oil over medium heat. When hot, add onion and garlic and sauté until translucent. Add squash and stir well. Add ketchup, tomato sauce and salt. Stir again. Cover and simmer over low heat until vegetables are tender.

VEGETABLE KISHKE

3/4 cup light tasting olive oil
2 stalks celery, cut into pieces
2 carrots, cut into pieces
1 onion, quartered
2 cloves garlic
1-1/2 cups whole wheat pastry flour
1-1/2 tsp. sea salt
1 tsp. paprika

Preheat oven to 350 degrees. Combine oil and vegetables in a food processor. Process until a thick paste is formed. Add flour and seasonings and process further. Shape into a roll onto a large piece of greased foil. Roll tightly in foil and bake on baking sheet for 1-1/2 hours at 350 degrees. Unroll, slice and serve. This may also be put into the cholent wrapped in foil, then unrolled and sliced when cholent is served.

CRACKER KISHKE

1 package Wasa or Ryvita Rye Crackers
2 stalks celery, cut into pieces
3 carrots, peeled and cut into pieces
1 onion, quartered
3 cloves garlic
3/4 cup light tasting olive oil
1 tsp. paprika
1 tsp. sea salt

Preheat oven to 375. Place all ingredients into a food processor and process until it forms a thick and smooth dough. Shape into a roll onto a large piece of greased foil. Roll tightly in foil and bake on baking sheet for 40 minutes. Unroll, slice and serve. This may also be put into the cholent wrapped in foil, then unrolled and sliced when cholent is served.

FARFEL 🌾

1 package of whole spelt farfel
1 large Spanish onion
5 cloves of garlic, minced
1-1/2 tsp. of salt
dash of pepper
dash of paprika
3 Tbsp. light tasting olive oil

Heat oil. Add onion and garlic and sauté for a few minutes. Add farfel and spices and sauté until browned. Add water to cover and cook until tender, approximately 15 minutes.

HOMEMADE BAKED BEANS

1 lb. Great Northern white beans
2 tsp. salt
1 (15 oz.) can of tomato sauce
2 Tbsp. apple juice concentrate
2 tsp. alcohol-free maple flavoring (optional)
1 medium onion, peeled
2 whole cloves

Cover beans with water and soak overnight. In the morning, drain beans. Place in a 3 quart saucepan with fresh water to cover. Bring to a boil and cook until beans are just soft, about 1 hour. Add salt after 45 minutes. Drain liquid from beans and reserve. Preheat oven to 325 degrees.

Combine tomato sauce and apple juice concentrate (and maple extract if desired). Add 1 cup of reserved cooking liquid.

Place beans in a greased 2 quart casserole and cover with sauce mixture. Stick the two cloves into the onion and put into the beans. Cover.

Bake for 5 to 6 hours until sauce is thick and syrupy and beans are soft. Remove onion and serve.

This can also be made in the crockpot. Soak the beans as stated and then place all the ingredients into the crockpot and cook on low heat for at least 8 hours. If you like things spicy, you can add some hot mustard to the sauce.

VEGETABLES & SIDE DISHES

KUGELS PUDDINGS

WHOLE WHEAT FRUIT NOODLE KUGEL

12 oz. package of whole wheat or brown rice noodles
4 eggs, beaten
1/4 cup canola oil
1/2 cup crushed pineapple in its own juice
4 apples thinly sliced with peel on it
1/4 cup unsweetened applesauce
1/4 tsp. cinnamon
1/2 tsp. sea salt
optional: 1/2 cup chopped nuts with some reserved for topping

You can substitute any other type of canned fruit for the pineapple, just make sure it is in its own juice and has no added sugars.

Cook noodles per package instructions, drain and set aside. Cool for 15 minutes. Preheat oven to 350. In a large bowl combine all ingredients, except noodles, mix well. Add noodles. Pour into greased 9" x 13" pan and bake for 45 minutes.

APPLE KUGEL

CAKE:
3 cups whole wheat pastry flour
1 jar banana baby food
1 cup light tasting olive oil
4 eggs
1 1/4 tsp. baking powder
1/2 cup orange juice

Mix all ingredients together very well.

FILLING:
10 cortland apples, grated with peel left on
1/2 tsp. cinnamon
1 tsp. vanilla

Spread half the cake mixture into a greased 9" x 13" pan. Spread the apple filling over it. Pour remaining cake mixture over apple filling and spread evenly. Bake at 350 for 1 hour and 15 minutes.

Optional: place half of cake mixture in bottom of pan, 3/4 of apple filling, remaining cake mixture and then the remaining 1/4 of apple mixture on top.

POTATO KUGEL

12 large white potatoes, scrubbed well, unpeeled
8 eggs
3/4 cup light tasting olive oil
1 Tbsp. salt
1 tsp. cream of tartar
1 grated onion (optional)

Heat oven to 400 degrees. Pour oil into a 9" x 13" pan. Place pan in oven to heat the oil. Beat eggs well. Add salt and cream of tartar. Using food processor, use kugel blade (smallest grating holes) and grate potatoes. Add potatoes to egg mixture. Blend well. Add onion, if desired. Pour into heated pan and place in oven, turn heat down to 350 degrees. Bake for 2 hrs or until golden brown on top.

LOKSHEN (NOODLE) KUGEL

This is my sons' favorite kugel, Aaron even likes to eat it cold. You can eliminate the strawberry fruit spread if you want the kugel to be less sweet. You can also vary the topping. I have substituted 1/4 cup of coconut or 1/4 cup chopped almonds for the cornflake crumbs.

12 oz. whole spelt medium noodles or brown rice
    noodles
1/4 cup light tasting olive oil
4 eggs, beaten
1/2 cup applesauce
1/4 cup strawberry fruit spread
1/2 cup chopped walnuts
4 apples, grated
1 Tbsp. cinnamon
1 tsp. alcohol-free vanilla extract
1-1/2 tsp. salt

TOPPING:

1 tsp. cinnamon
1/4 cup sugar-free cornflake crumbs

Preheat oven to 350 degrees. Cook noodles until tender. Drain and place in a bowl. Mix noodles with oil and set aside to cool. Meanwhile, beat together eggs, applesauce, walnuts, apples and seasonings. Mix well. Add noodles to egg/apple mixture. This can be baked in a greased 9" x 13" pan, 2 - 1 lb loaf pans or 5 small kugel pans.

Mix cinnamon and cornflake crumbs. Sprinkle on top of kugel(s). Cover and bake for 50 minutes. Uncover and bake for 10 more minutes.

SWEET CHALLAH KUGEL

1-1/2 lbs leftover whole wheat challah, dried out
1 cup orange or apple juice
1/2 cup soy, oat or almond milk
6 eggs, beaten
1 large jar banana baby food
1/4 cup light tasting olive oil
1 Tbsp. alcohol-free vanilla extract
3/4 tsp. sea salt
2 Tbsp. cinnamon
2-3 medium sized apples, grated

Preheat oven to 350 degrees. Break up dried challah into small pieces. Pour the juice and milk over the challah and soak it until it is softened. Add eggs, bananas, oil, vanilla, salt and cinnamon. Mix well. Add grated apples and mix again. Bake in a greased 9" x 13" pan for 50 minutes. Serve warm.

CARROT KUGEL

1/2 cup Earth Balance margarine
1 medium mashed banana
1 egg, beaten
3 Tbsp. orange juice
1-3/4 cup whole wheat pastry flour
1 tsp. baking powder
1/2 tsp. baking soda
1 tsp. sea salt
1/2 tsp. cinnamon
1/2 cup chopped walnuts
2 cups grated carrots

Preheat oven to 350 degrees. Cream margarine and banana together until smooth. Add egg, juice, flour, baking powder, baking soda, salt, cinnamon and nuts. Mix well. Add carrots and mix again. Place in a 9" greased round pan. Bake for 40 minutes. Serve warm or room temperature.

SWEET POTATO KUGEL

1 cup unsweetened apple sauce
3/4 cup oat milk
1 tsp. cinnamon
3/4 tsp. nutmeg
1/2 tsp. sea salt
3 eggs, beaten
6 sweet potatoes (4 cups grated, peeled)

Preheat oven to 350 degrees. Combine all ingredients except sweet potatoes in a large mixing bowl. To prevent discoloration of the potatoes, add the sweet potatoes to the egg mixture as quickly as possible. Mix all ingredients very well and pour into a greased 1-1/2 quart casserole dish. Bake for 20 minutes. Stir once and continue baking an additional 40 minutes or until top is browned and the edges pull away from the sides of the casserole dish.

BROCCOLI KUGEL

You can use zucchini or cauliflower instead of the broccoli. For a really pretty three layer kugel, you can triple this recipe and make one third with broccoli, one third with cauliflower and one third with sweet potato.

1 lb. broccoli, chopped (fresh or frozen)
3 eggs, beaten
3/4 cup mayonnaise
1/4 cup whole wheat flour OR
    2 Tbsp. oat flour plus 2 Tbsp. brown rice flour
2 Tbsp. dried chopped onion
2 tsp. salt
1 Tbsp. garlic, chopped

Mix all ingredients together, place in a greased 9" round pan and bake in 350 degree oven for 40-45 minutes.

DAIRY

CAULIFLOWER STUFFED POTATOES

4 large baking potatoes, unpeeled
1 small head of cauliflower
12 oz. low fat cottage cheese
2 Tbsp. Dijon mustard
paprika, optional for garnish

Scrub potatoes well and pierce with a fork on all sides. Bake unwrapped potatoes at 350F for one hour or until skins are crispy and insides are soft. Towards the end of the hour, steam cauliflower until tender (but not mushy). Set aside.

In a medium sauce pan, combine cottage cheese and mustard, stir over low heat until cheese is melted. Scoop out pulp of potatoes, setting aside the shells. Mix potatoes with cheese and mustard. Add cauliflower to potato mixture and mix lightly. Stuff potato mixture back into shells, sprinkle with paprika, bake for another 10-15 minutes, until tops are lightly browned.

SPINACH AND CHEESE

1 package fresh spinach
1 container low fat cottage cheese
1 onion, chopped
1 clove garlic, minced
1 Tbsp. minced onion
1 tsp. mustard
1/4 cup skim milk

Wash and check spinach very thoroughly. Steam spinach or simmer with very little water until tender. Set aside. In saucepan, mix remaining ingredients. Stir until cheese is melted. Add spinach, stir over low heat 3-5 minutes. Serve hot.

CREAM OF SPINACH

This recipe is very versatile. You can use it as a side dish, as a stuffing for chicken, as a filling for crepes or as an omelet filling.

1/2 lb. fresh spinach
1 small onion, diced
1-1/2 Tbsp. light tasting olive oil
1 Tbsp. oat flour
3 Tbsp. milk (cow's, oat or soy)
salt and pepper to taste

Wash and dry spinach. Tear into small pieces. Sauté onion in oil until translucent. Add flour and gradually add the milk. Add spinach, salt and pepper and simmer for 5 minutes.

SPINACH BAKE

1 onion, chopped
1 tsp. light tasting olive oil
2 packages frozen chopped spinach, thawed
4 eggs, beaten
1 c. milk
1 c. whole wheat bread crumbs OR
    rye cracker crumbs (see misc. section)
2/3 cup parmesan cheese, grated
1 tsp. oregano
1 tsp. basil
1 tsp. garlic, minced
2 tsp. sea salt
1/2 tsp. pepper

Sauté chopped onion in oil until browned. Mix all ingredients well and pour into a greased 9" baking pan. Bake at 350 degrees for 30 minutes or until a toothpick inserted into the middle comes out clean.

CHEESE BLINTZES

4 eggs, beaten well
1 cup milk
1 cup whole wheat pastry flour
1/4 tsp. salt

FILLING:
1 lb. farmer cheese
2 egg yolks
2 Tbsp. apple juice concentrate
1 Tbsp. alcohol-free vanilla extract

Mix eggs and milk together in a blender. Add flour and salt and blend well until there are no lumps. Spray an 8" non-stick pan with non-stick spray and between frying each blintz. Pour a small amount, a bit less than 1/4 cup, of blintz batter into the hot pan and twirl pan around so the batter covers the bottom of the pan. This is the way to make a really thin blintz! Fry until it pulls away from the sides or until it solidifies on the edges. Then flip over and fry for only 3-4 seconds. Set aside. Makes approximately 12 blintzes.

Combine all filling ingredients. For each blintz, put about 2 Tbsp. of filling in the middle of the pancake on the golden brown side. To roll up, fold up the bottom over the filling, then fold in the left and right sides and continue to roll up from the bottom to the top. These can be eaten cold or fried in a little butter and served warm.

BANANA BLINTZES

4 eggs, beaten well
1 cup milk
1 cup whole wheat pastry flour
1/4 tsp. salt

FILLING:
3 oz. cream cheese, softened
1/3 cup cottage cheese
2 tsp. cinnamon
1 tsp. alcohol-free vanilla extract
3 ripe bananas
2 Tbsp. butter
sour cream for topping

Mix eggs and milk together in a blender. Add flour and salt and blend well until there are no lumps. Spray an 8" non-stick pan with non-stick spray and between frying each blintz. Pour a small amount, a bit less than 1/4 cup, of blintz batter into the hot pan and twirl pan around so the batter covers the bottom of the pan. This is the way to make a really thin blintz! Fry until it pulls away from the sides or until it solidifies on the edges. Then flip over and fry for only 3-4 seconds. Set aside. Makes approximately 12 blintzes.

Blend cream cheese, cottage cheese, cinnamon and vanilla. Dice one banana and fold into the mixture. For each blintz, put about one rounded tablespoon of filling in the middle of the pancake on the golden brown side. To roll up, fold up the bottom over the filling, then fold in the left and right sides and continue to roll up from the bottom to the top. These can be eaten cold or fried in a little butter and served warm. Slice remaining bananas. Top each blintz with sour cream and sliced bananas.

SMILEY FACE PANCAKES

1-3/4 cup milk
2 eggs
1 tsp. alcohol-free maple extract
2 cups whole wheat pastry flour
2 tsp. baking powder
1 tsp. sea salt
sliced or slivered almonds to make the smiley face

Mix together all liquid ingredients. Add dry ingredients and mix just until combined well. In a greased or sprayed non-stick frying pan or griddle, pour about 1/6th cup of batter per pancake for smaller size or 1/3 cup of batter per pancake for larger size. Immediately place almonds to make a smiley face. When pancake bubbles, flip and cook other side for 1 to 2 minutes.

You can experiment with different nuts to create the faces you want, just make sure they are not heavy nuts or it will not work. You can also make other expressions, i.e. sad, angry, monster, etc.

RANCH DRESSING

1/2 cup mayonnaise
1/2 cup buttermilk
2 tsp. parsley
1/2 tsp. sea salt
2 cloves garlic, crushed
1/2 tsp. paprika
1 tsp. onion, minced
1/4 cup grated parmesan cheese

Mix all ingredients in a blender. Refrigerate for a few hours before serving.

DAIRY

CREAMY CHEESE DRESSING

3 oz. cream cheese, softened
1/2 cup mayonnaise
1/4 cup milk
1 Tbsp. garlic, crushed
7 oz. feta cheese, crumbled
4 Tbsp. parmesan cheese, grated

Using an electric mixer, beat together all ingredients. Chill for a few hours before serving.

SQUASH & BROCCOLI CASSEROLE

2 lbs yellow squash, sliced
2 lbs broccoli florets, cut into bite sized pieces
1 large onion, chopped
3 cloves garlic, crushed
1 Tbsp. butter, for sautéing
4 Tbsp. butter
3 large eggs, beaten
1 cup mayonnaise
4 cups cheddar cheese
1 tsp. sea salt
3 cups ground almonds

Steam broccoli and squash separately until crisp-tender, about 5-8 minutes. Sauté onion until translucent, set aside. Mash squash and butter together. Stir in broccoli, garlic, eggs, onion, mayonnaise, and cheese. Spoon into two lightly greased 2 quart baking dishes. Sprinkle with almonds.Bake at 350 for 20-25 minutes or until golden.

CHEESE LASAGNA

1 box whole wheat or brown rice lasagna noodles
6 cups marinara sauce – sugar-free
1 lb. textured vegetable protein crumbles
    (rehydrated)
2 cups mozzarella cheese, grated
1 cup parmesan cheese, grated
1 lb. ricotta cheese – part skim or skim

Preheat oven to 375 degrees. Add textured vegetable protein crumbles to the marinara sauce and cook for 5 minutes. Layer ingredients in a 9" x 13" pan as follows: 1/2 cup marinara sauce, uncooked noodles, 1-1/2 cups marinara sauce, 8 oz. ricotta cheese, 2/3 cup mozzarella cheese, and 1/4 cup parmesan cheese. Again, layer uncooked noodles, pressing them into the cheese, 1-1/2 cups marinara sauce, 8 oz. ricotta cheese, 2/3 cup mozzarella cheese, 1/4 cup parmesan cheese and uncooked noodles. Top that with the remaining marinara sauce, mozzarella and parmesan cheeses. Bake for 55 minutes.

If you are using brown rice lasagna noodles, check the lasagna about 25 minutes into baking as the noodles can tend to poke up out of the sauce. Just gently press them down with a fork and continue baking.

BROCCOLI AND WILD RICE CASSEROLE

1 Tbsp. butter
1 large Spanish onion, chopped
1 cup red pepper, chopped
2 cloves garlic, crushed
2 Tbsp. butter
2 Tbsp. whole wheat or brown rice flour
2 cups milk
2 cups cheddar cheese, grated
2 Tbsp. hot and spicy mustard
1-16 oz. package of frozen broccoli florets, thawed
1 cup cooked wild rice
4 Tbsp. parmesan cheese, grated (optional)

Preheat oven to 350 degrees. Sauté onions, red peppers and garlic in 1 Tbsp. butter until soft. Set aside. Make a roux by heating the butter in a saucepan over medium heat. When melted and bubbling, add flour, mixing quickly and well. Slowly add milk, stirring constantly. When mixture has thickened, add cheddar cheese and mix well until cheese is fully melted. Add mustard, broccoli and rice and mix well. Pour into a greased 2 quart baking dish. Sprinkle the top with parmesan cheese, if desired. Bake 30 minutes.

QUICHE 🌾

PIE CRUST:
1-1/4 cup whole wheat pastry flour
1/4 tsp. sea salt
5 Tbsp. Earth Balance margarine or butter
6 Tbsp. iced cold water

Combine flour and salt in a mixer bowl. Cut margarine into flour with a pastry blender (or 2 forks) until the mixture resembles coarse meal. Stirring with a fork, gradually add the cold water just until the dough is moistened and holds together when pinched between your fingers. You may not need all of the water. Gather up the dough and cover. Refrigerate for at least one hour or up to 24 hours. Roll out the dough into a large circle about 1/8" thick. Place into an ungreased deep 9" pie plate.

FILLING:
1 cup Swiss cheese, shredded
8 slices soy strips (soy bacon - optional) – cooked
    and crumbled
1/3 cup onion, chopped
1 Tbsp. crushed garlic
4 large eggs
2 cups milk (regular, oat or soy) or for a splurge,
    2 cups heavy cream
1/4 tsp. sea salt
1/4 tsp. white pepper

Preheat oven to 425 degrees. Sprinkle cheese and soy over the prepared crust. Chop onion into very fine pieces. Sprinkle onion and crushed garlic over the cheese and soy. Beat eggs well and add all the rest of the ingredients and beat to combine. Pour into a 9" pie plate. Bake for 15 minutes. Reduce heat to 300 degrees and bake for about 30 more minutes or until a toothpick inserted into the center comes out clean. Let stand for a few minutes before serving.

PIZZA

DOUGH:
2-1/2 cups whole wheat or whole spelt flour
1 package dry yeast
1–1/4 cups warm water
3/4 tsp. sea salt

Dissolve yeast in warm water. Stir in the flour and salt. Beat well, with a fork, about one minute. Let rise about 1-1/2 hours. Preheat oven to 425 degrees. Grease two cookie sheets or two pizza pans. Divide dough in half and roll each piece out into 11" circles. Prebake crust for 10 minutes. Remove crust from oven.

SAUCE:
2 cans tomato sauce
1 Tbsp. oregano
1 Tbsp. crushed garlic
1 Tbsp. minced onion
1 tsp. basil
1/2 tsp. black pepper

Mix the tomato sauce and spices. Divide in half and spread each half over one of the prepared crusts.

TOPPING:
12 oz. shredded pizza cheese blend (cheddar and
     mozzarella)
1/2 cup grated parmesan (optional)

Divide cheeses in half and sprinkle over the prepared crusts and sauce. Bake for about 10 minutes until cheese is melted and bubbly.

Optional: You can add any of the following vegetables on top of the cheese:

Broccoli (blanched)
Red peppers, thinly sliced
Tomatoes, thinly sliced
Spinach, chopped
Mushrooms, blanched and thinly sliced

Once you try making your own pizza, you will never go back to the store bought ones. You can vary the pizza to suit your personal tastes. You can even add some textured vegetable protein crumbles (TVP or dried soy) to give the pizza a stronger protein boost. For a wheat-free alternative, use 1-1/4 cups oat flour plus 1-1/4 cups brown rice flour instead.

DAIRY

73

CABBAGE, APPLE & CHEDDAR SLAW

DRESSING INGREDIENTS:

1/4 cup balsamic vinegar
2 Tbsp. light sesame oil
2 tsp. Dijon mustard
1 tsp. soy sauce
1/2 tsp. cinnamon
2 Tbsp. light tasting olive oil
Salt, preferably sea or kosher, to taste
Freshly ground black pepper to taste

SALAD INGREDIENTS:

1 medium cabbage, cored and thinly sliced (about 8 cups)
3 apples (any variety), unpeeled, cored and cut into matchsticks
3 medium carrots, peeled and coarsely grated (about 2-1/2 cups)
2 celery stalks, cut into matchsticks
1 cup grated extra sharp cheddar
1/2 cup chopped toasted walnuts

In a blender, combine vinegar, sesame oil, mustard, soy sauce and cinnamon; blend until smooth. While blender is running, slowly add oil.
Season with salt and pepper. Set aside. In a large bowl, combine all salad ingredients. Add enough dressing to coat salad well and toss together until well combined. Cover and refrigerate until serving time.

BLUE CHEESE DRESSING

8 oz. whipped cream cheese
1 cup mayonnaise
1/2 cup milk
7 oz. kosher blue cheese

With an electric mixer, whip together the cream cheese, mayonnaise and milk. Add the blue cheese, crumbling it as you mix. Beat well until combined.

FISH

HOMEMADE SALMON GEFILTE FISH

4 lbs. ground salmon (purchase already ground)
8 eggs
3 onions, grated very finely
6 cloves garlic, crushed
4 carrots, grated
3 Tbsp. salt and 2 tsp. pepper
2 onions, halved
2 cloves of garlic
1 Tbsp. sea salt and 1/2 tsp. pepper

Combine salmon through 2 tsp. pepper in a food processor. Mix on high speed until completely ground up and mixed well, about 5 minutes. Prepare parchment paper, approximately 16" x 18", by moistening it with water. Place desired amount of fish mixture onto the parchment paper and roll up into a loaf. The loaves may be frozen for future use. Makes about 6 loaves.

Fill a large pot half way with water. Add rest of ingredients, and bring to a boil. Add wrapped loaf to boiling water and cook for 2 hours. Cool and serve. If you prefer balls, you can shape the mixture into balls and, using wet hands, place gently into the boiling water (as above) and continue to cook as directed.

EASY GEFILTE FISH & SLICED FISH

1 frozen gefilte fish loaf, no sugar added
4 slices of white fish, carp or salmon
2-3 fresh carrots, peeled, whole
1 large onion, sliced
1 whole head of garlic, crushed
1 tsp. salt
pepper to taste
water to cover

Put all the fish in a pot and add the rest of the ingredients. Bring to a boil and then simmer for 1-1/2 hours. Let cool completely before removing from pot.

Refrigerate for a few hours, preferably overnight. Slice gefilte fish loaf and serve one slice of fish along with a slice of gefilte fish.

This is a really easy supper. If you have picky eaters, you can serve the fried fish without the tomato sauce. If you are avoiding wheat, you can substitute 1 cup of finely ground rye cracker crumbs for the matzo meal.

GEFILTE FISH IN TOMATO SAUCE

1 frozen gefilte fish roll, no sugar added
1 cup of whole wheat matzo meal
2 Tbsp. garlic powder
1 Tbsp. salt
light tasting olive oil, for frying
1 (8oz.) can tomato sauce

Defrost roll slightly. Slice into 10 pieces. Mix matzo meal with seasonings. Dip each piece of fish into the matzo meal. Fry in oil until light golden brown on each side. Transfer to 9" x 13" pan. Add tomato sauce and bake for 30 minutes.

TUNA OR SALMON PATTIES

2 (7 oz.) cans tuna OR 1 (15-1/2 oz.)can of salmon
1 large potato, boiled with skin on – must be warm
3 eggs
2 tsp. sea salt
2 Tbsp. garlic powder
1 small onion, minced
light tasting olive oil, for frying

With an electric mixer on medium speed, beat together tuna, warm potato and eggs. Add seasonings and onion and beat until combined. Shape into medium sized patties. Fry over medium heat in a little bit of oil. Drain well on paper towels.

BAKED SALMON

4 salmon fillets
2 Tbsp. garlic powder
4 Tbsp. Dijon mustard
1 Tbsp. light tasting olive oil
2 Tbsp. unsweetened ketchup

Place fillets on a lightly greased baking pan. Mix rest of ingredients and spread on salmon. Bake at 350 degrees for 1/2 hour or until fish flakes with a fork.

SALMON WITH DILL SAUCE

4 salmon fillets
2 tsp. garlic powder
2 tsp. onion powder
sea salt to taste

Preheat oven to 350 degrees. Mix together the garlic and onion powders. Sprinkle 1 tsp. of the mixture on each fillet. Salt to taste. Place fillets on a lightly greased baking pan. Bake for 1/2 hour or until fish flakes with a fork. Alternatively, the fish can be broiled or grilled until cooked through. When cooked, place a fillet on a platter with a dollop of dill sauce. Serve immediately

DILL SAUCE:
1/2 cup mayonnaise
1/4 cup hearty mustard
1/2 cup fresh dill
sea salt to taste

Mix all ingredients in blender. Chill for 6 hours to allow flavors to blend.

FRIED FLOUNDER

1/2 cup whole wheat flour
1 cup whole wheat or whole grain dry bread crumbs
2 Tbsp. garlic powder
2 tsp. sea salt
1 Tbsp. paprika
2 eggs, beaten
1 lb. flounder fillets
light tasting olive oil, for frying

Mix bread crumbs and spices together. Dip flounder in flour and then in egg and then pat into bread crumb mixture. Fry in oil until golden brown on each side. Drain well on paper towels.

BATTER-FRIED FISH

1-1/3 cups whole wheat **OR** whole spelt flour.
2 tsp. baking powder
2/3 tsp. salt
3 Tbsp. plus 1 tsp. butter
1 lb. sole or flounder
1/2 tsp. black pepper
1 tsp. garlic powder
1 tsp. onion powder
1 large egg, beaten
1 cup club soda or seltzer
oil for frying

For a wheat free alternative use 2/3 cup brown rice flour and 2/3 cup oat flour

Mix flour(s), baking powder, salt and spices. Cut in butter with a pastry blender or two forks until it resembles fine crumbs. Set aside.

Heat oil in deep fryer to 375 degrees. Rinse fish and pat dry. Combine flour mixture, egg and club soda to make a thick batter. Dip fish into the batter. Deep fry fish, a few pieces at a time for about 5 minutes or until it is deep golden brown and the fish flakes easily. Drain on paper towels.

TUNA TACOS

2 (7 oz.) cans tuna
1/2-1 package of taco seasoning, no sugar added,
    depending on taste
1/3 cup hot water
1/2 cup shredded cheddar cheese
Taco shells
Salsa, no sugar added
Sour cream

Heat nonstick pan over medium heat. When warm, add flaked tuna. Sprinkle the taco seasoning over the tuna and add hot water. Stir well until heated through. Fill each taco shell with 2 Tbsp. tuna mixture, top with cheddar cheese, salsa and sour cream.

This is a kid friendly recipe. My boys love when I serve all the toppings on the side in small bowls and they can assemble their own tacos. The toppings can include: cheese, salsa, cut up tomatoes and sour cream. For an even more exciting look, you can use blue corn taco shells.

TUNA NOODLE CASSEROLE

1/4 cup butter
1 small red pepper, chopped
1 small onion, chopped
1 cup sliced fresh mushrooms
1/4 cup whole wheat flour
2-1/2 cups milk
2 cups shredded cheddar cheese
3 (7 oz.) cans tuna, drained and flaked
12 oz. package whole wheat flat noodles or brown
    rice pasta
2 tsp. dried parsley flakes
1 tsp. sea salt and 1/2 tsp. pepper
1 tsp. garlic powder
1/2 cup finely ground almonds
2 Tbsp. butter, melted

Preheat oven to 350 degrees. Precook noodles according to package directions. Melt butter in a large skillet over medium heat; add bell pepper, onion and mushrooms and sauté 5 minutes or until tender. Add flour to vegetable mixture and stir well. Slowly add milk and cook, stirring constantly, until thickened, about 5 minutes. Remove from heat. Add cheese, stirring until melted. Stir in tuna, whole wheat pasta, and seasonings; spoon into a lightly greased 9" x 13" baking pan. Bake covered for 25 minutes. Stir together almonds and melted butter. Sprinkle over casserole and bake 5 more minutes.

MEAT & CHICKEN

YUMMY ROAST

Any type of kosher roast
    (shoulder, French, square tip, top of rib, minute)
Sliced onions equal to 1/2 the weight of the roast
    (e.g. 2 lbs. onions for 4 lb. roast)
1 whole head of garlic, crushed
Salt to taste
    (kosher meat is pretty salty to begin with so I
recommend salting at the end)

Braise meat in an oiled pot. Add the rest of the ingredients
and barely cover with water. Bring to a boil and then
simmer, covered for 3-4 hrs. Remove roast from pot, cool
and slice. Using a hand blender (or transfer the liquid into
a food processor once it has cooled), blend the liquid that is
left in the pot. All the onions and garlic make a terrific sauce
for the meat.
Crock-pot variation: Same as above but add only 1/4 cup
of water. Cook on low for 8-10 hours.

BBQ RIBS

4-1/2 lbs beef ribs
BBQ Sauce (see below)

Heat oven to 325 degrees. Place ribs into a large roasting
pan. Pour sauce over ribs and cover and bake until tender,
about 2-1/2 hours. Spoon sauce over ribs and serve.

BBQ SAUCE
(thanks to Sheila B. for this sauce recipe)
2 Tbsp. dry mustard
2 Tbsp. chili powder
1/4-1/2 tsp. cayenne pepper
    (more if you like a lot of heat)
2 Tbsp. paprika
2 Tbsp. garlic powder
2 Tbsp. onion powder
2-1/2 tsp. salt-free lemon pepper
2 tsp. ground cinnamon
1 tsp. ground allspice
1 tsp. sea salt
6 Tbsp. apple juice concentrate
1 (15 oz.) can tomato sauce

Mix all ingredients together.

This sauce can be used for BBQ chicken. We absolutely adore this recipe and the best part is that you can make it as mild or as hot as you like. Just adjust the amount of cayenne pepper. Any extra sauce that didn't come in contact with raw meat can be refrigerated for about a week

SIMPLE CHICKEN

4 chicken leg quarters
1 medium onion, diced
2 cloves garlic, crushed
2 Tbsp. paprika
sea salt to taste (optional)
1 Tbsp. water

Heat dry frying pan over medium-high heat. Add onion and garlic and sauté 2 minutes. Sprinkle chicken on both sides with paprika and salt. Add chicken to onion and garlic, skin side down. Add about 1 Tbsp. of water to the bottom of the pan. Cover tightly. Lower heat and simmer chicken for 1-1/2 hours or until tender
Optional: At the end of cooking, remove the cover and increase the heat to high. Watch the chicken carefully as it can easily burn. Remove the chicken from the heat when the sauce is reduced by half. Spoon the sauce over the chicken and serve.

CHINESE STYLE PEPPER STEAK

1-1/2 lb.pepper steak
    (thinly sliced beef chuck, fat removed)
2 Tbsp. light tasting olive oil
2 cloves garlic, crushed
1/2 tsp. salt (optional)
1/4 tsp. ground black pepper
1/4 cup soy sauce (check the label!)
1 cup fresh bean sprouts
1 cup canned tomatoes, diced
2 green peppers, seeded and cut into strips
1/2 cup fresh mushrooms, sliced
1 Tbsp. cornstarch
2 Tbsp. cold water
4 green onions, sliced

Brown the steak in the oil either in a skillet or in the slow cooker if you can sauté in it. If you used a skillet, transfer the steak into the crock pot. Combine garlic, salt, pepper and soy sauce and pour over the steak. Cook on low for 6 - 8 hours. Turn the control to high. Add bean sprouts, tomatoes, green peppers and mushrooms. Dissolve cornstarch in water, stir into the pot. Cover and cook on high 15-20 minutes or until thickened. Sprinkle with green onions and serve over brown rice.

STUFFED CHICKEN BREASTS

4 boneless, skinless chicken breasts
1/2 lb. fresh mushrooms
1/2 lb. fresh spinach, washed and drained
4 Tbsp. light tasting olive oil
1/2 cup chopped onion
2 cloves garlic, crushed
1/2 tsp. crushed oregano leaves
pinch of black pepper
1 tsp. salt (optional)
1/4 cup chicken broth

Rinse, pat dry and chop mushrooms. Set aside. Barely wilt spinach by steaming it in a minimum amount of water for a few minutes. Drain well, squeezing out excess water. Chop (should make about 1/2 cup). Set aside. In a large skillet, heat 2 Tbsp. of the oil until hot. Add onions and mushrooms. Sauté until tender, about 4 minutes. Add garlic, oregano, pepper, salt and spinach. Cook and stir well for 1 minute. Set aside to cool.

Meanwhile, flatten each chicken breast, placing them between 2 sheets of wax paper or plastic wrap, pound with a mallet until about 1/4" thick. Spoon 1/4 of the mushroom/spinach mixture onto the center of each chicken breast. Roll lengthwise. Secure with toothpicks.

Place rolled chicken breasts into a 9" square pan. Combine chicken broth with remaining 2 Tbsp. of oil. Spoon over chicken. Bake uncovered, basting frequently, until chicken is tender, about 15 - 20 minutes. Sprinkle with chopped parsley before serving (optional).

You can make the mushroom/spinach mixture the night before and refrigerate. Let it come to room temperature before using. You can also use the spinach filling to stuff chicken leg quarters, just lift up the skin and push the spinach mixture inside.

MEAT & CHICKEN

87

FRUITY CHICKEN

3 lbs chicken, in quarters or eighths
1/2 lemon, sliced
juice from 1/2 lemon
1/2 grapefruit, in sections
1 orange, in sections
juice from 1 orange
2 Tbsp. granulated garlic
pepper and salt to taste

Place chicken pieces in a large roasting pan. Sprinkle with garlic, salt and pepper. Combine juices and fruit sections. Pour over chicken. Cover well. Bake in 350 degree oven for 1 hr 10 minutes. Uncover pan. Bake an additional 20 minutes, basting often.

SPICY CHICKEN WRAPS

1-1/2 pounds skinned, boned chicken breast,
      cut into 1/2" strips
2 tsp. chili powder
2 tsp. light tasting olive oil
1-1/2 tsp. ground cumin
1/2 cup Sour Supreme (tofu pareve sour cream)
1/4 cup mayonnaise
2 Tbsp. minced fresh parsley
2 Tbsp. fresh lime juice
2 garlic cloves, crushed
4 (8") whole wheat, corn or brown rice tortillas
3 cups chopped romaine lettuce
1-1/3 cups chopped seeded tomato
2 jalapeno peppers, seeded and diced (optional)

Combine the chili powder, oil, cumin and chicken in a heavy-duty zip-top plastic bag, seal and shake to coat. Combine the Sour Supreme with next 5 ingredients in a small bowl and whisk. Sauté chicken in oil in a large nonstick skillet over medium-high heat for 2 minutes or until chicken is done. Add the Sour Supreme mixture; cover and cook 1 minute. Remove from heat.

Warm the tortillas according to the package directions. Spoon about 3/4 cup chicken mixture onto each tortilla, and top each serving with 3/4 cup chopped lettuce and 1/3 cup chopped tomatoes (and 1/2 of a jalapeno pepper, if desired). Roll up wrap.

STUFFED CABBAGE

3 Tbsp. light tasting olive oil
2 Tbsp. whole wheat flour
1 (46 oz.) can tomato juice
4 Tbsp. tomato paste
1 cup apple juice
1/2 cup water
1 Tbsp. sea salt
2 large turkey necks (optional)
1 large head of cabbage
1-1/2 lbs ground turkey
1/2 cup uncooked brown rice
1 Tbsp. light tasting olive oil
1 medium onion, minced
4 cloves garlic, crushed
1 beaten egg

This traditional recipe is usually very sugary. The turkey necks make a really thick and savory sauce that is so good you won't miss the sugar. If you have any leftover meat, you can shape them into balls, drop them into the boiling sauce and serve them as meatballs.

Freeze cabbage head. Once defrosted, the leaves will come off very easily and are easy to check for bugs.

Heat oil in pot, stir in flour to make a roux. Add rest of ingredients, including any leftover chopped cabbage. Bring to a boil and cook for a few minutes. While it is cooking, combine turkey, rice, oil, onion, garlic and egg. Place 1 Tbsp. mixture on each leaf and roll up (place meat on end towards stem, turn stem over meat, fold in sides and then roll up). Add stuffed cabbage rolls one by one to the boiling sauce. Lower the heat and cook on low for 2 hours.

GARLIC CHICKEN

3 lb. chicken, cut into quarters or eighths
1 head of garlic, crushed
2 Tbsp. paprika
cooking spray

Preheat oven to 350 degrees. Rub the crushed garlic all over the chicken, place in ungreased roasting pan. Sprinkle the paprika over the garlic chicken. Spray the chicken pieces with cooking spray. Cover well. Bake for 1 hr and 10 minutes. Uncover and bake an additional 20 minutes.

APRICOT CHICKEN

3 lb. chicken, cut into quarters or eighths
2 Tbsp. fruit sweetened apricot preserves
2 Tbsp. mayonnaise
2 Tbsp. sugar free ketchup (or tomato sauce)
2 Tbsp. dried chopped onion
1 Tbsp. sea salt

Mix all the ingredients (except chicken). Spread the sauce over the chicken and cover. Bake at 350 for 1 hr and 10 minutes. Uncover and bake an additional 20 minutes.

SWEET BAKED CHICKEN

6 lb. chicken, cut into eighths
2 eggs, beaten
2 Tbsp. water
1 cup whole wheat matzo meal
1 tsp. salt
1/8 tsp. pepper
1/2 tsp. garlic powder
1/2 cup light tasting olive oil
1/2 cup hot water
1/4 cup unsweetened apple butter
1 cup orange juice

Remove chicken skin. Trim pieces of all excess fat and pat dry. In a shallow bowl, combine eggs and water. Beat well. In another shallow bowl, combine matzo meal, salt, pepper and garlic. Dip chicken in egg mixture, then roll in matzo meal.

Fry chicken in oil over medium heat until golden brown, approximately 5 minutes per side. Remove chicken to an ungreased Dutch oven or covered roasting pan.

In a small bowl combine hot water, apple butter and orange juice. Pour over chicken and cover. Bake in preheated 325 degree oven for 45 minutes or until tender. Baste occasionally.

CONDIMENT CHICKEN

3 lb. chicken, cut into quarters or eighths
4 Tbsp. sugar free ketchup
4 Tbsp. Dijon mustard or spicy mustard
1 Tbsp. garlic powder

Mix ketchup, mustard and garlic powder.
Spread it over the chicken pieces and bake at 350 for 1-1/2
hours, covered.
Optional: boneless, skinless chicken breasts can be used.
Bake uncovered at 375 for 1/2 hour.

ALMOND SCHNITZEL

2 lbs boneless, skinless chicken cutlets, pounded flat
1 cup ground almonds
1 Tbsp. garlic powder
2 tsp. sea salt
2 eggs, beaten
light tasting olive oil for frying

Mix almonds, garlic and salt. Dip cutlets into egg and then
pat into almond mixture. Fry in oil over medium heat until
golden brown on each side. Drain well.

I first used this recipe as a Pesach schnitzel (you can do that, too). However, it is so delicious and my family likes it so much, I serve it all year round. Of course, it is perfect for those that are trying to avoid wheat or other flours

MUSHROOM CHICKEN

6 lbs. chicken, cut into quarters or eighths
3 cups soy or oat milk
3 cups chicken broth
1 red pepper, chopped
1 orange pepper, chopped
1 yellow pepper, chopped
2 cups fresh mushrooms, sliced
4 cloves fresh garlic, crushed

Heat soy milk, chicken broth, vegetables and garlic in a large dutch oven. When it comes to a boil, add chicken and lower heat to a simmer. Simmer over medium heat for 1-1/2 hours. If the gravy is not thick enough, after removing the chicken pieces, add some cornstarch and let it simmer to thicken. This is really good served over brown rice.

TURKEY FRIED RICE

1 cup bean sprouts
1 Tbsp. light tasting olive oil
1 cup mushrooms, sliced
3 cups cooked brown rice
1 cup smoked turkey or cooked turkey,
    cut into bite sized pieces
2 Tbsp. green onions, thinly sliced
1 Tbsp. light tasting olive oil
2 large eggs, slightly beaten
3 Tbsp. tamari or soy sauce
1/8 tsp. white pepper

Rinse bean sprouts and drain. Heat oil in frying pan over medium heat. Cook mushrooms for about 1 minute. Add bean sprouts, rice, turkey and onions. Cook over medium heat for about 5 minutes, stirring constantly. Push the rice mixture to the side of the skillet. Add the oil and add the beaten eggs, stirring constantly, until the eggs are thickened but still moist. Combine eggs and rice then stir in the soy sauce and pepper.

STUFFED CAPON

4 lb capon
10 oz. brown rice
1 Tbsp. sugar free soy sauce
2 oz. slivered almonds, roasted
1 Tbsp. paprika
salt & pepper to taste
2 Tbsp. light tasting olive oil
2 Tbsp. paprika
4 cloves garlic, crushed
sea salt, to taste

Cook rice according to package directions. During the last 10 minutes of cooking time, add soy sauce, paprika, salt and pepper. Let cool. Mix in almonds. Brush capon with a mixture of oil, paprika, garlic and salt. Dry the inside cavity of the capon. Stuff it with the rice-almond mixture. Cover roasting pan and roast at 350 degrees for 2-1/2 hours or until tender and cooked through. Uncover and bake another 10 minutes to brown the skin.

CHICKEN, HOT DOG & POTATO DISH

7 Wise Chicken Hot Dogs (or other brand no sugar
        added hot dog), cut into bite sized pieces
5 oz. boneless, skinless chicken breasts,
        cut into bite sized pieces
1 Tbsp. light tasting olive oil
1 white potato, skin on, cubed
1 sweet potato, peeled and cubed
1 medium onion, cubed
2 cloves garlic, crushed
2 Tbsp. spicy brown mustard
water to cover

Heat oil in a medium saucepan. Add potatoes, onion and garlic and sauté for about 5 minutes. Add the hot dogs and chicken breast. Add mustard and water to cover and stir well. Continue cooking over medium heat until the chicken is cooked through and the potatoes are soft, about 20 minutes.

SWEET POTATO CHICKEN

3 lb. chicken, cut into quarters or eighths
4 large sweet potatoes, peeled and thinly sliced
1 large Vidalia or Spanish onion, chopped
2 cloves garlic, crushed
4 Tbsp. light tasting olive oil
4 Tbsp. bold and spicy mustard
1/4 cup orange juice
1 orange, sliced

Preheat oven to 375 degrees. Place sweet potatoes and onions on the bottom of an ungreased roasting pan. Place chicken on top and rub the chicken with the crushed garlic. Combine oil, mustard and orange juice and pour it over the chicken. Cover and bake for 1 hour, basting often. Uncover chicken, place orange slices on top of the chicken and bake for another 15 minutes.

PICNIC FRIED CHICKEN

8 chicken leg and thigh portions
1 cup oat flour
1 cup brown rice flour
2 cups fine cornmeal
2 Tbsp. Old Bay seasoning
1 Tbsp. chili powder
salt and pepper, to taste
2 cups oat milk or soymilk
2 Tbsp. vinegar
light tasting olive oil for frying

Combine flours, cornmeal and seasonings. Combine oat milk and vinegar. Soak the chicken in the oat milk mixture for 2 minutes. Remove, draining off excess liquid. Coat the chicken in the flour/cornmeal mixture. Let sit for 30 minutes before frying. Heat oil to 325 degrees. Deep fry chicken about 15 minutes (watch carefully as larger pieces need more time than smaller pieces). Cool and refrigerate overnight. Pack up and go on your picnic!

CHICKEN POT PIE

Pie Crust (see below)

1 package (10 oz.) frozen peas and carrots
1/3 cup light tasting olive oil
1/3 cup whole wheat pastry flour
1/3 cup chopped onion
2 Tbsp. minced garlic
1/2 tsp. sea salt
1/4 tsp. pepper
1-3/4 cups chicken broth
2/3 cup oat milk , almond milk or soy milk
3 cups cut-up cooked chicken

PIE CRUST:
2-1/2 cups whole wheat pastry flour
1/2 tsp. sea salt
2/3 cup Earth Balance margarine
3/4 cup ice water

Combine flour and salt in a mixer bowl. Cut margarine into flour with a pastry blender (or 2 forks) until the mixture resembles coarse meal. Stirring with a fork, gradually add the cold water just until the dough is moistened and holds together when pinched between your fingers. You may not need all of the water. Gather up the dough and cover. Refrigerate for at least one hour or up to 24 hours.

Rinse the frozen vegetables in cold water to separate; drain. Heat oil in a 2 quart saucepan over medium heat. Stir in flour, onion, garlic, salt and pepper. Cook, stirring constantly, until mixture is bubbly; remove from heat.

Stir in broth and oat milk. Heat to boiling, stirring constantly. Boil and stir one minute. Stir in chicken and peas and carrots; remove from heat. Heat oven to 425 degrees. Roll out two-thirds of the prepared pastry into a 13" square. Ease into a 9" square pan. Pour chicken mixture into the pastry lined pan.

Roll out the remaining pastry into an 11" square. Place pastry over chicken mixture and turn the edges of the pastry over and flute. Pierce pastry top with a fork to vent. Bake for about 35 minutes or until golden brown.

For wheat allergies, you can substitute 3 Tbsp. oat flour and 2 1/2 Tbsp. brown rice flour for the 1/3 cup whole wheat pastry flour and omit the pie crust. This is a great recipe for leftover soup chicken.

CHOLENT

1 large onion, chopped
2 cloves garlic, crushed
6 Tbsp. paprika
1/2 cup barley
1-1/2 cups soaked and rinsed navy beans
2-1/2 lbs. of any of the following:
    stew meat, cholent meat with bones, skinless
    chicken breasts or thighs, bone on
water to cover
salt and pepper to taste after it is cooked

Sauté onions and garlic. Add barley and beans and sauté a few minutes. Sprinkle with paprika and mix well. Add meat and then water to cover. Cook for at least 3 hours on low. Put on blech for Shabbos.

CHICKEN & WILD RICE CASSEROLE

3/4 cup brown rice
1/4 cup wild rice
1/4 cup light tasting olive oil
1 small onion, chopped
4 cloves garlic, minced
1/4 cup whole wheat flour OR
    2 Tbsp. brown rice flour and 2 Tbsp. oat flour
1-1/2 cups chicken broth
3 cups chopped cooked chicken
1-1/2 cups soy milk, oat milk or almond milk
1 (6 oz.) can sliced water chestnuts, drained
1 (4-1/2) oz. jar sliced mushrooms, drained
1 Tbsp. chopped fresh parsley
2 tsp. sea salt and 1/2 tsp. pepper
2-1/2 oz. sliced almonds

Combine brown and wild rice. Add 2-1/2 cups water and cook, simmering until tender, about 50 minutes. Set aside. Heat oil in a Dutch oven over medium-high heat. Add onion and sauté until tender. Add garlic and mix. Add flour and cook, stirring constantly, 1 minute. Add broth and cook, stirring constantly, 1 to 2 minutes or until mixture is thickened and bubbly. Stir in rice, chicken, soy milk, chestnuts, mushrooms, parsley, salt and pepper. Spoon into a lightly greased 11" x 7" baking dish. Top with sliced almonds. Bake at 350 for 15-20 minutes or until thoroughly heated.

I always had a hard time finding a great recipe that would use up all my leftover boiled chicken. This recipe does a super job of using up those leftovers and providing us with a terrific all in one meal.

LAMB TAGINE

3 lbs boneless lamb shoulder or stew meat,
    cut into 1-1/2" pieces
2 Tbsp. light tasting olive oil
1/2 tsp. salt
1/2 tsp. freshly ground black pepper
1 large yellow onion, coarsely chopped
1/3 cup fresh Italian parsley, chopped
1/4 cup fresh cilantro, chopped
1 tsp. cinnamon
1 tsp. ginger
1/8 tsp. crushed saffron threads
2 cups chicken broth
2 Tbsp. apricot fruit spread
1-3/4 cups canned chick-peas, rinsed and drained
2 oranges, peeled and cut into sections
1/4 cup sliced almonds, toasted
1-1/2 cups whole wheat couscous, prepared
    according to package directions

For wheat allergies, you can substitute brown rice for the couscous.

Heat the oil in a heavy Dutch oven over medium-high heat. Season the lamb with salt and pepper. In batches, add the lamb to the Dutch oven, searing about 4 minutes or until just browned. Using a slotted spoon, transfer each batch of lamb to a bowl. Add the onion to the Dutch oven and sauté until tender, about 4 minutes. Mix in the parsley, cilantro, cinnamon, ginger, saffron and chicken broth. Return all of the lamb with its juices to the Dutch oven and bring to a rolling simmer. Cover and reduce the heat to low, simmer until lamb is tender, about 1-1/2 hours.

Add the apricot fruit spread and chickpeas to the lamb mixture, stir to incorporate. Simmer until heated through, about 15 minutes. Transfer to a deep platter and garnish with orange sections and almonds. Serve over the couscous.

DESSERTS

CHEESECAKE (DAIRY)

CRUST:
1 cup rolled oats
1/2 cup almonds
1/2 cup pecans
2 Tbsp. sugar free grated coconut
2 Tbsp. vanilla
2 Tbsp. cinnamon
6 Tbsp. butter

This recipe makes two 8" cheesecakes.

Toast all ingredients, except butter, at 350 degrees in a pan for about 15-20 minutes until golden. Process the mixture in a blender or food processor until finely chopped. Separate into two 8" pans. Add 3 tablespoons of melted butter to each pan and mix well. Press into pan to form crust.

FILLING:
3 (8oz.) packages of cream cheese (the block type)
1 jar banana baby food
    (or 1/2 cup of mashed fresh banana)
4 eggs
1 teaspoon vanilla

This is my most requested dessert recipe. The trick for using banana is to either use the baby food or to puree the banana in a food processor or blender until it is completely smooth.

Soften cream cheese. Whip cream cheese with beaters until smooth. Add eggs and banana and vanilla. Beat well until smooth and creamy. Pour cheese mixture in crust-lined pans, dividing the cheese equally. Bake at 375 degrees for 30 minutes.

TOPPING:
1 pint sour cream
2 teaspoons vanilla
4 Tbsp. mashed banana
    (or 4 Tbsp. from banana baby food)

Stir sour cream, vanilla and banana together. Spread over baked cheese filling, again dividing the sour cream equally between the two pans. Bake at 375 degrees for 20 minutes.

NON-DAIRY CHEESECAKE (PAREVE)

CRUST:
1 cup rolled oats
1/2 cup almonds
1/2 cup pecans
1/4 cup peanuts
2 Tbsp. sugar free grated coconut
2 Tbsp. vanilla
2 Tbsp. cinnamon
6 Tbsp. light tasting olive oil

This recipe makes one 10" cheesecake

Toast all ingredients, except oil, at 350 degrees in a pan for about 15-20 minutes until golden. Process the mixture in a blender or food processor until finely chopped. Place oat/nut mixture into a 10" cheesecake pan and add 6 tablespoons of oil and mix well. Press into pan to form crust.

FILLING:
2 (8 oz.) containers of tofu cream cheese
    non-hydrogenated only
3 eggs, beaten
1 T. vanilla
1 T. strawberry all fruit spread
1 jar banana baby food (or 1/2 cup of mashed fresh
    banana – use a blender)

Cream tofu cream cheese and eggs. Add vanilla, strawberry all fruit and banana and cream until smooth. Pour onto prepared crust. Bake at 350 for 50 minutes to 1 hour, until top is golden and middle is firmly set.

BANANA CAKE

2-1/4 cups whole wheat pastry flour
3/4 cup oat milk
3/4 tsp. baking soda
1/2 tsp. salt
4 oz. Earth Balance margarine, softened
3 ripe bananas, mashed
1 tsp. vanilla
2 eggs
1/2 cup chopped walnuts (optional)

With an electric mixer, beat all ingredients together and bake in a 9" x 13" pan at 350 degrees for 35 minutes.

CINNAMON BUNS 🌾

DOUGH:
2 packages dry yeast
1-1/2 tsp. salt
6-1/2 to 7 cups whole wheat pastry flour
1-1/4 cups apple juice
1/2 cup apple butter
1 cup butter or Earth Balance margarine
3 eggs, at room temperature
1/2 tsp. vanilla extract

In a large mixer bowl, combine yeast, 1/4 cup apple butter, salt and 2 cups of flour. In a 1 quart saucepan, heat the remaining 1/4 cup apple butter, apple juice and butter until warm. Butter does not have to melt. Gradually add warm liquid to the above yeast ingredients, beating with mixer at low speed. Increase speed to medium and beat 2 minutes. Add eggs, vanilla and 2-1/2 cups of flour. Beat 2 more minutes. By hand, stir in enough additional flour to make a stiff dough, about 2 cups. Turn dough onto a lightly floured board and knead 8 to 10 minutes until smooth and elastic, adding more flour if necessary. Place dough in well-oiled bowl and turn to oil the top. Cover and let rise in warm place about 1 hour until doubled in bulk. Punch down, turn onto floured board, cover with bowl and allow to rest 15 minutes for easier shaping.

To make buns:
1/2 Recipe of Dough (see above)

FILLING:
3/4 cup apple butter
1/2 cup chopped walnuts or pecans
1-1/2 tsp. cinnamon
1/4 cup light tasting olive oil

Prepare Dough recipe. Grease baking sheet.
Combine all filling ingredients, except oil, in a small bowl. Place dough on a floured board. Roll dough into a 18" x 12" rectangle. Brush with oil and spread the apple filling mixture over the dough. Starting with the 18" side, roll dough jelly-roll fashion, pinch seam to close. With seam side down, cut roll crosswise into 18 slices. Pinch outer sides together on the bottom of each bun - the center will puff up and filling won't run out. Place on a baking sheet. Cover and let rise about 40 minutes until doubled in bulk. Preheat oven to 400 degrees and bake for 20 minutes. While buns are warm, you may brush them with apple juice concentrate.

APPLESAUCE CAKE

1 cup Earth Balance margarine, softened
1 jar banana baby food
2 eggs
1 (32 oz.) jar of natural applesauce
4 cups whole wheat pastry flour
1 Tbsp. baking soda
2 tsp. cinnamon
1 tsp. ground cloves
1/2 tsp. salt
1 cup finely chopped walnuts

Preheat oven to 325. Cream margarine and bananas. Add eggs and mix well. Pour in applesauce, beating well, then add dry ingredients. Fold in nuts.

Pour batter into a greased 9" x 13" pan and bake for about 1 hour or until toothpick inserted into middle comes out clean.

Make a cake by baking in a 9 " round cake pan for about 20-25 minutes. You can then frost it with the whipped cream frosting found in the miscellaneous section. If you need to avoid wheat, you can substitute the wheat flour with 1 cup oat flour and 1/2 cup brown rice flour.

CAROB MUFFINS

1 jar banana baby food
    (or 1/2 cup mashed banana)
3 Tbsp. light tasting olive oil
1 egg
1 cup oat milk
1 tsp. alcohol-free vanilla extract
1-1/2 cup whole wheat pastry flour
1/4 cup carob powder
1-1/4 tsp. baking soda
1 Tbsp. baking powder
1/2 cup shredded coconut

Preheat oven to 350. Beat the banana, oil and egg until creamy. Add in the milk and vanilla extract. Stir in the remaining ingredients and mix until just combined. Spray nonstick muffin pan with cooking spray. Fill each cup 2/3 full. Bake for 13-15 minutes until the tops spring back when touched.

"CHOCOLATE" BALLS

1 cup almond butter
1 cup apple butter
3/4 cup carob powder
1 cup shredded coconut

Mix all ingredients together by hand and form small balls.
Refrigerate.

BLUEBERRY CORN MUFFINS

1 cup yellow cornmeal
1 cup whole wheat pastry flour
1 Tbsp. baking powder
1/4 tsp. sea salt
4 Tbsp. apple juice
2 eggs
1-1/4 cups oat milk
1/4 cup light tasting olive oil
1 cup blueberries, fresh or frozen

Preheat oven to 400. In a mixing bowl, combine all the dry
ingredients. Make a well in the center. In another bowl,
combine all the liquid ingredients. Add the liquid
ingredients to the dry ingredients and mix just until
combined. Do not over mix. Gently fold in blueberries,
avoid over mixing. Spray a nonstick muffin pan with
cooking spray. Fill each cup 2/3 full. Bake 15-20 minutes
or until a toothpick comes out clean.

RUGELACH

2-1/2 lbs whole wheat pastry flour (about 10 cups)
1 lb. Earth Balance margarine
1-1/2 oz fresh yeast
1-1/4 cup warm apple juice
2 eggs
4 egg yolks
1/2 tsp. salt
1 beaten egg (to brush rugelach)

Preheat oven to 350. Mix 1 lb flour with margarine. Set aside. In a separate bowl, dissolve yeast in apple juice. Add remaining flour and rest of ingredients and mix. Combine the yeast mixture with the margarine mixture and knead until smooth. Divide into 6 parts. Cover dough and set to rise for 20 minutes. Roll out each part into a large circle about 1/8" thick. Cut into 16 wedges. Add filling and roll up from the wide end towards the narrow end. Brush with beaten egg. Place onto a nonstick cookie sheet or a lined regular sheet. Leave space between each piece for them to rise. Bake for 18 minutes.

FILLING OPTIONS:

1) 1 cup all fruit spread, 1/2 cup ground walnuts (2 Tbsp. cinnamon optional). Mix well and spread onto each triangle before rolling up. You can also substitute coconut for walnuts.
2) 1 cup apple butter, 1/2 cup carob powder, 1/4 cup coconut. Mix well and spread onto each triangle.
3) 1/2 cup almond butter, 1/4 cup chopped almonds, 1 cup apple butter. Mix well and spread onto each triangle before rolling up.

Spread filling <u>thinly</u> over the dough.
Optional: You can roll each section into a rectangle, approximately 12" x 9", spread the filling over the entire rectangle and roll up from the bottom (the longest side) into a log shape. Slice the log, placing each piece on the cookie sheet and baking as above.

PECAN PIE

PIE DOUGH:

1-1/4 cup whole wheat pastry flour
1/4 tsp. sea salt
5 Tbsp. Earth Balance margarine or butter
3 Tbsp. ice cold apple juice
3 Tbsp. ice water

Combine flour and salt in a mixer bowl. Cut margarine into flour with a pastry blender (or 2 forks) until the mixture resembles coarse meal. In a small bowl, mix the cold apple juice and the water together. Stirring with a fork, gradually add the cold apple juice/water mixture just until the dough is moistened and holds together when pinched between your fingers. You may not need all of the cold apple juice/water mixture. Gather up the dough and cover. Refrigerate for at least one hour or up to 24 hours. Roll out the dough into a large circle about 1/8" thick. Place into 9" inch pie plate.

FILLING:

1-1/2 cups pecans
2 Tbsp. whole wheat pastry flour or oat flour
10 Tbsp. Earth Balance margarine or butter, softened
2/3 cup apple juice concentrate
1 Tbsp. alcohol free maple flavoring
2 eggs

Preheat oven to 375 degrees. In a food processor, blend the pecans and flour until finely ground. In a separate bowl, mix the softened margarine, apple juice and extract. Beat in the eggs, mix well. Beat in the pecan/flour mixture. Pour into pie shell and bake for 40-50 minutes, until filling is golden brown. You may have to shield the crust to avoid burning.

JELLO

You can use any juice & fruit combination. For example apple juice with pear chunks or grape juice with halved grapes or orange juice with banana chunks.

1 package unflavored unsweetened jel
    (check label some diet ones have sweetener
    or some unflavored ones have sugar)
2 cups mixed berry juice, no sugar added
1 cup blueberries or strawberries

Bring juice to a boil, remove from heat. Slowly sprinkle the jel over the juice, mixing well to make sure there are no lumps. Alternatively, you can use a hand blender to mix it well. After it is mixed, add the fruit and chill until firm.

HAMENTASHEN

4 cups whole wheat pastry flour
4 eggs
1 jar banana baby food (large size - stage 3)
1 cup Earth Balance margarine
1 Tbsp. orange juice
2 tsp. baking powder
1 tsp. vanilla
Pinch of salt
Apple butter for filling

Soften margarine. Preheat oven to 350 degrees. Grease cookie sheets or use parchment paper (I used parchment).

You can also use fruit only spread instead of apple butter or even peanut butter.

Place all ingredients in a large mixer bowl and beat together until the dough is smooth. Roll into a ball and refrigerate until firm, covering completely in plastic wrap. Divide into four parts.On a well-floured board, roll out each portion to about 1/8" thick. Using a 2" round cookie cutter, cut out circles. Place 1/2 tsp. of apple butter on each circle.To shape into a triangle, lift up the right and left sides and have them meet in the center above the filling. Bring the top flap down to the center to meet the two sides. Pinch edges together. Bake for 20 minutes at 350 degrees.

Makes about 6-1/2 dozen cookies.

PESACH CHOCOLATE CAKE

4 whole eggs
1 cup apple syrup (see note)
2 medium bananas, mashed
1 cup light tasting olive oil
1/4 cup cocoa
1/2 cup walnuts, chopped
3/4 cup potato starch
6 oz. ground almonds

Beat eggs until mixed well, not frothy. Add the rest of ingredients mixing only until combined. Do not over mix. Pour into 9" x 13" pan. Bake at 350 degrees for 40-45 minutes or until center comes out clean with a toothpick.

To make the apple syrup, boil one jar of apple juice in a heavy bottomed saucepan until reduced by half. Let the syrup come to room temperature before using in any of the recipes. You can refrigerate any leftover syrup for one week.

PESACH NUT CAKE

12 eggs, separated
1/3 cup apple syrup (see note)
6 oz. ground almonds
1 medium banana, mashed
6 Tbsp. apple syrup (see note)

Preheat oven to 350 degrees. Whip egg whites until stiff. Slowly add 1/3 cup apple syrup and keep beating until stiff. In a large bowl, beat together the egg yolks, almonds, banana and 6 Tbsp. apple syrup. Fold the whites into the egg yolk mixture and gently pour into a 9" x 13" pan. Bake for 50 minutes.

PESACH COOKIES

4 egg whites
1/8 tsp. salt
1/4 cup apple syrup (see note)

Preheat oven to 225 degrees. Beat egg whites until stiff. Add salt and apple syrup and continue to beat until very stiff. Place batter into a storage bag that has a hole cut in the corner (to make a pastry bag). Pipe cookies out onto a parchment lined cookie sheet, forming rounds. Place immediately into oven. Bake until very dry, about 1 hour and 20 minutes.

CHERRY BUCKLE

BATTER:
1 cup apple juice
1/4 cup Earth Balance margarine
2 eggs
2 cups whole wheat pastry flour
2 tsp. baking powder
1/2 tsp. sea salt
1/2 tsp. cinnamon
2 cups fresh, tart cherries, washed and pitted

TOPPING:
1 cup sliced almonds
1/2 tsp. cinnamon
1/4 cup Earth Balance margarine

Mix apple juice, margarine and eggs. Stir in dry ingredients. Fold in cherries. Spread batter into a greased 9" square pan. Mix topping ingredients together until crumbly. Sprinkle on top of batter, pressing into batter. Bake at 375 for 40-45 minutes.

You can use 3 cups of fresh fruits to substitute for the pineapple. A terrific berry recipe: 2 cups of strawberries and 1 cup of blueberries. Use whatever fruit is in season.

PINEAPPLE ICE CREAM (DAIRY)

1 ripe pineapple, cut up into chunks
Juice from 1 small orange
1-1/2 cups heavy whipping cream

In a blender, combine half of the pineapple chunks with the juice from the orange. Blend until liquefied. Then add the rest of the pineapple and blend until it becomes very smooth. Pour the pineapple mixture into two quart size freezer bags. Store bags flat in the freezer and freeze until it is slushy, about 1-1/2 hours. Whip the cream (best to chill the beaters and bowl a few minutes in the freezer before whipping) until it is stiff. In a large bowl, stir in the pineapple slush into the whipped cream and mix well. Return to freezer until completely frozen, about 1 hour. Serve.

BANANA COCONUT PUDDING

3 cups oat milk
3/4 cup millet
1 tsp. salt
1 cup shredded unsweetened coconut
1 ripe banana, mashed
1 tsp. alcohol-free vanilla extract

Bring oat milk to a boil, add millet and salt and cover.
Simmer on low for 40 minutes. Turn off heat and set aside
for 30 minutes. Add the coconut, banana and vanilla, stirring
well. Pour into 6 custard cups and serve hot or warm.

MAPLE ALMOND OATIES

1/2 lb Earth Balance margarine (2 sticks)
2 eggs
1 cup mashed banana
1-1/2 Tbsp. cinnamon
1-1/2 Tbsp. alcohol-free maple extract
2 cup whole wheat pastry flour
1/2 tsp. sea salt
2 tsp. baking powder
3 cup old fashioned rolled oats
1/2 cup unsweetened shredded coconut
1-1/2 cups slivered almonds

*These cookies do
not expand in the
oven. They are
wonderfully
crunchy and a
great treat for the
children.*

Preheat oven to 350 degrees. Cream the margarine and egg
together until well blended and smooth. Gradually beat in
the banana, cinnamon and maple extract. Mix well until all
ingredients are well blended.

In a large bowl, mix the flour, salt, baking powder, oats,
coconut and almonds. Using a wooden spoon, combine the
dry ingredients until they are blended well and evenly
distributed. Stir the dry ingredients into the margarine/egg
mixture and mix thoroughly until there is no sign of dryness.

Cover two large cookie sheets with parchment paper. Drop
heaping tablespoons of the dough onto the cookie sheets,
about 2" apart and press down lightly to flatten. Bake for 20
minutes or until lightly browned. Cool on a wire rack. Makes
about 2-1/2 dozen cookies.

HALVAH

1/2 cup shredded **unsweetened coconut**

1/2 cup **ground almonds**

1/2 cup **wheat germ**

1/2 cup **sesame butter**

1/2 cup **banana baby food (or mash a ripe banana
and then blend to a smooth consistency)**

2 Tbsp. strawberry **fruit spread (fruit sweetened
only, no sugar/sweetener added)**

Mix all ingredients very well. With moistened hands, form
into small balls. Freeze until firm and then serve. Store in
refrigerator.

MISCELLANEOUS

WHOLE GRAIN DRIED BREAD CRUMBS

6 slices of whole grain bread

Preheat oven to 250 degrees. Place slices on a cookie sheet and bake. Turn bread over once during baking.   It takes approximately 45 minutes until bread is completely dried out on both sides. Place into food processor and process dried bread until it becomes fine crumbs. Use in place of white bread crumbs in your favorite recipes.

If you are allergic to wheat, you can substitute rye cracker crumbs for the bread, omit the baking and continue the recipe as stated above.

WHOLE WHEAT MATZO MEAL

One box of whole wheat matzo

Break up 3-4 matzos at a time and place in food processor. Keep processing matzo until it is so finely ground it resembles flour.

ALMOND BUTTER

1-1/2 cups almonds, can be raw or roasted
2 tsp. sea salt

Process almonds and salt in food processor. Keep processing it on high until it gets thick and creamy. This takes quite a long time, about 40 minutes. Refrigerate.

MISCELLANEOUS

115

MAYONNAISE

1 cup light tasting olive oil
1 egg
1 tsp. lemon juice
1/4 – 1/2 tsp. sea salt, to taste

Mix egg, lemon juice and salt in a blender or food processor. Slowly add the oil, drop by drop. One trick that helps is to poke a small hole in the bottom of a paper or plastic cup, place the empty cup in the feed shoot of the food processor and pour the oil into the cup, it will slowly drip out of the hole at the bottom of the cup.

Prepared mayonnaise not only has sugar, but also uses oils that are not as healful as olive oil. For a stronger taste, you can use pure virgin olive oil.

ROASTED ALMONDS

2 cup raw almonds

Preheat oven to 400 degrees. Place almonds in a large roasting pan. Roast for about 10 minutes or until the almonds start to smell like popcorn. This same method can be used for walnuts, pecans and most other nuts.

GARLIC & ONION ALMONDS

2 cup raw almonds
1 egg white
1 Tbsp. garlic powder
1 Tbsp. onion powder
1 tsp. sea salt

Preheat oven to 325 degrees. Whisk egg white until it is white and foamy. Add spices and blend. Add almonds and toss to coat. Place almonds on a parchment paper lined baking sheet, making sure to spread them out so they are in single layer. Bake for 10 minutes and toss well. Bake for an additional 10 minutes.

WHIPPED CREAM FROSTING

2 cup heavy cream
1 Tbsp. alcohol-free, sugar-free vanilla extract
1 mashed banana (to taste)

Chill bowl and beaters very well. Pour cream into chilled bowl and beat well until thickened. Add extract and banana, if desired, and whip until stiff. Use to frost cakes, especially great for a birthday cake.

To enjoy a whipped topping with lower fat content, combine 1/2 cup powdered skim milk, 1/2 cup iced water, 1 Tbsp. alcohol-free vanilla extract and 2 Tbsp. fresh lemon juice in a chilled bowl. With very chilled beaters and bowl, beat on high until peaks form, at least 7 minutes.

MISCELLANEOUS

INDEX

Challah p. 13
Pretzels & Onion Bread
p. 14, 15 (left)

Mini Corn Dogs p. 23 (top)
Suffed Baby Squash p. 21

Mahogany Chicken Wings p. 24 (left)
Split Pea & Barley Soup p. 27

Ministrone Soup p. 28
Cream of Asparagus Soup p.31(left)

Tomato Salad p. 38
Spinach Salad p.36 (top)

Cabbage & Rice p.47 (top)
Easy Marinated Bean Salad p. 37

Stuffed Acorn Squash p. 46

Four Colored Green Beans p. 48 (top)
Vegetable Kishke p. 53

Lokshen Kugel p. 60 (top)
Apple Kugel p. 59

Cheese Blintzes p. 67 (top)
Sweet Challah Kugel p. 61

Smiley Faced Pancakes p. 69
Cheese Lasagna p.71 (left)

Tuna Tacos p. 81
Gefilte in Tomato Sauce p. 78 (top)

Tuna Noodle Casserole p. 81 (top)
Almond Schnitzel p. 91

Stuffed Chicken Breast p. 87 (left)
BBQ Ribs p. 85

Maple Almond Oaties p. 111 (top)
Carob Muffins p. 104

Cheesecake p. 101